About "The Anatomy of Death: Notes from a Healer's Casebook"

Trained as a scientist initially, and then a hands-on healer, Elena Gillespie had no idea that her father's death would lead to a door that contravenes everything we think we know about death and dying from a Western perspective. Starting out with a promise to her father that she would learn everything she could about this journey to ease its difficulties for others, she approached her visionary experiences with the open mind of a researcher. This took her to places that few of us travel, but are long familiar to the medium, the psychic and the shaman of ages past. From the shuttered passings of her father and little Kevin, to the epiphanies gleaned from the White Tiger, Regina and the Twin Towers, this is the story of that discovery.

Reviews

'In your journey through life you may forget at times that you are a visitor on this planet earth. The finitude of life, however, will not let you put off forever your remembering the end of this physical existence – which must come sooner or later. Elena Gillespie can see beyond the time before you were born and after you pass through the portals at the nether end of life. Her stories – of what she has seen, and how the sharing of her far vision has helped many people to know there is a spirit path they will follow after their physical death – are a true delight and inspiration. This is a book you won¹t want to put down till you¹ve savored its every drop of wisdom.'

Daniel J Benor, MD
– Author of *Healing Research***, Volumes I-III**
Editor of open access *International Journal of Healing and Caring*
http://ijhc.org

'In this book, Elena Gillespie shares her experiences at the boundaries between our everyday world and a world of visions and spirits. Her writing opens up for each reader a new understanding of death as a critical part of human development, a spiritual passage, and not just an endpoint. I recommend this book for all human beings who wish to approach death more gracefully.'

Donald Moss, PhD, Chair, School of Mind-Body Medicine, and co-author of
Pathways to Illness, Pathways to Health http://amzn.to/15lyVZ6

'"The Anatomy of Dying: Notes from a Healer's Casebook" takes its readers on a remarkable journey that will challenge many of their cherished beliefs, whether they are committed atheists or members of a traditional religion. In her book, Elena Gillespie has presented stories from her practice as an "energy healer." Each story is eloquently written, emotionally moving, and engaging, providing unconventional but instructional perspectives on the end of Earthly life.'

Stanley Krippner, PhD, Alan Watts Professor of Psychology, Saybrook University; co-author "Personal Mythology." http://www.amazon.com/Ph.D.-Stanley-Krippner/e/B008RQVMKG/ref=ntt_dp_epwbk_0

The Anatomy of Dying: Notes From a Healer's Casebook

By Elena Gillespie PhD

To all my Teachers
and
for Steve, Nathaniel and Dylan

In the foothills of the Himalayas lives a tribe, the Naga, "The People." In their creation stories, The People tell of a falling away from the Divine, to be forever separated from it and doomed to walk this world alone. In one of their greatest Revelation stories, there is the promise that The People will again be rejoined with those they love who have passed before them, where the hills meet the clouds.

Chapters

Synopsis of Future Work
Copyright

Prologue

This book followed many long and winding paths, with many detours, blind alleys, unforeseen revelations and just plain accidents of fate. When I was in my twenties, I began study in conventional medicine intending to become a physician, but was confronted with questions about my own healing that seemed to have no rational answers. A frustrating period of struggle followed, during which I stumbled across a type of healing that, while used in other parts of the world for centuries, contradicts much of what we think we know about wellness.

In contrast, the model I encountered is based on the concept that the human body, indeed, everything that exists has an energy field. The foundation of this healing modality is that practitioners trained to recognize areas where the patient's energy field is stagnant, which manifest as physical illness, can alter this energy field and reestablish health.

The basics of this process are actually fairly easy to learn and nearly everyone can learn it. It goes under many names, Qi-Gong, Reiki, Therapeutic Touch, spiritual healing, a myriad of other titles and has been used for millennia in other parts of the world.

Even a lifetime of study in this area may only yield a rudimentary understanding of its use. Some healers are born with their abilities fully developed, but most people have latent abilities that grow stronger with training and practice. The predominant view in Western culture does not give much credence to these kind of skills, but we are the exception, not the rule. The more I study current theories in physics and ontology about how the nature of reality and interfacing consciousness might be constructed, the less wild this model becomes. Having said that, we do not presently have the technology to measure the medium of healing itself, all we can do is measure the effects, and even that, not well. How it works is unknown, so therefore its effects are most likely influenced by a number of variables we just don't understand yet.

So then, what is this book about? In conducting NIH-funded research in Reiki for chronic pain and in my own private practice as an energy healer, I found that some people who came for Reiki immediately got better, some recovered slowly over time, and others did not. Others met with that final door we call death progressing through a distinct set of steps common to all of them, but in a relaxed and joyous way. How and why was this? In the course of their dying process, what had we done that was different?

Over time, I have been given glimpses of a larger picture, through my own lens of understanding. Our predominantly positivist belief system was never meant to answer any of these questions about life after death, and sometimes our religious faith falls short when we come to that door ourselves; of course, we are only human. Our perspective is so limited by our essentially materialist mentality and yet, it doesn't have to be this way. Over the centuries, other cultures have left interesting written records of the existence of other layers of consciousness that manifest in the dying process.

Dr. Elizabeth Kubler-Ross' work was among the first in the West to outline the emotional passages a person experiences before dying. Her stages of denial, anger, bargaining, depression and finally acceptance revolutionized the way the terminally ill are cared for, leading to the beginning of the hospice movement in the United States. Not all patients go through these passages, but when they do, acceptance can evolve to enlightenment for both the patient and their families.

The Buddhists have studied these processes over centuries and possess a finely tuned understanding of the function and meaning of death within their culture. For them, death is merely a punctuation mark, a single brushstroke in a much larger picture that goes on forever. It's all well and good that the Eastern perspective has come to such resolution about this process, but in a culture that worships youth and believes science has the answer to everything, how can death be looked at as anything other than a defeat?

I am primarily a storyteller, after a lifetime in the hard sciences, I now believe it is our stories that hold the ultimate power to transform. So this book is a collection of stories on my path of learning about these processes with those patients who passed through that final door. Though I have been given permission both by the patients and their families to tell these stories, their names and even some of the extraneous facts have been changed to protect their privacy.

Still, the people and their stories do not constitute all of my experience; as time went on, the view of the interface of death and life was presented to me in more universal terms. As they seemed to have relevance to the topic, I have included these stories as well. This book is not about me, but when the student is ready the teacher appears, as the saying goes, and each of these people and experiences appeared at a time in my life that not only added to my knowledge about dying, but also taught me how to live.

These stories are not meant as a proof one way or the other that an afterlife exists because there is no such proof; each person has to come to their beliefs about this in their own way. It is an invitation to reexamine old ideas, to see if it can help you in facing these passages. Since we will all be terminally ill at the end of our lives, yet we are also destined to live, it is meant as a handbook for all of us. So as well as to my teachers, it is to us that I dedicate this book.

Elena Gillespie PhD

Winter 2014

Beginnings

My mother died when I was 11 years old, so my relationship with my father evolved into the usual struggle between a widower who had children late in life and a willful firstborn girl child. He didn't know what to do with me and I made a career out of not letting him find out. It was the clash of the titans, but by young adulthood the teenage angst had dropped away and he had become a central anchor in my life.

My father was a quiet, extremely intelligent man who, after recovering from the shock of having two children to raise by himself, set to accomplishing this task by completely suppressing his dreams. An artist by nature, he honed his skills in stained glass after his surgery, but he had spent his professional life in a job that he hated to support his family.

When I was 25 years old and immediately after his retirement, my father called on a Saturday afternoon. In the midst of his usual sparse 'Everything's fine' conversation, he abruptly told me he was to have three-quarters of his stomach removed the following Tuesday. He had been diagnosed with cancer, the same illness that had ended his own father's life. The announcement came like breaking glass, I realized it doesn't take much to bring it all crashing in. Now began a long tunnel whose dark finish we knew would come no matter what we did.

A brief respite accompanied by a ticking clock followed the surgery, then a blur of hospitals and doctors, frustration and an overriding anxiety, and finally, two years later, the bedridden end. Those who have dealt with the wasting, prolonged illness of someone they love know this terrain. His physician was a wonderful, caring man who did all that he could to support my father's wishes, but this was 1981 and the available choices were limited.

My father chose to stay at home during the last part of his illness. Two weeks before he died, his doctor came to the house and told my father that he believed we were immortal, that it was time to think about that next stage, to let go and leave this one behind. My father refused all food and medication from that point onward. At the time, I was enraged at what his doctor had done, I felt he was interfering in a process where he had no right to meddle, but now I understand what the doctor did was necessary to relieve my father's suffering, which at that point was terrible.

In 1981, hospice care in the United States was not yet widely established. The medical community considered it barely acceptable to "allow" a patient to die at home. There were virtually no legal means of effectively controlling pain for a patient who wanted to do this. Morphine skin patches or intravenous pumps were not yet in general use, and only a nurse or physician could administer injectable painkillers. There were simply no regulations in place to allow it. A request like this was looked on with suspicion as being an attempt by an addict to obtain narcotics, but with someone in my father's condition, addiction was clearly no longer an issue. We knew he would never regain his health so as not to need it anymore, and oral medication was not strong enough to help him. We were in a place where there was no relief for any of us.

Struggling to honor what my father wanted, his doctor enrolled him in a research project that allowed us to administer methadone to him orally. A synthetic form of heroin, methadone is fairly effective as a means of pain control. However, trying to cajole a semi-conscious patient to swallow an oral liquid is close to impossible, and the chances of aspirating liquid into the lungs and causing pneumonia are very great. I seriously doubt we got enough in him to make much difference; most of it ended up on him or the bedclothes. Days and nights degenerated into a maze of pill bottles, attempting to keep him clean and comfortable, and the thousand other things that a patient needs, all without the proper resources.

My sister, my uncle, and myself were a sad, desperate little trio who just sort of stumbled through a minute at a time. Picture looking at the crest of a mountain that you absolutely have no idea how to scale, yet you know you must climb; you try not to think about it because you know there is no turning back, you just climb. We were trapped in a medical system that by its own claim was the most sophisticated in the world, and my father lay dying in the most barbaric pain imaginable. I was consumed by a black rage; it stalked me like a panther, everywhere, in my dreams at night. I could have killed him to relieve his suffering and anyone trying to prevent me, had I the means. Yet in the end it was not a decision I had to make.

My father died at 6:00 o'clock on the evening of his 69th birthday. All of us had left the room for a moment. It was a door he wanted to go through by himself, he did not want us to suffer any more. Never before had I taken such an emotional hit, nor have I since. Still, in the fog that settled in afterwards, I felt a sense of relief, he was finally free. That night I also hit a milestone, I drank a fifth of whiskey by myself.

Looking down at his tortured body from the foot of the bed that night, I vowed that no one in my care, or my sphere of influence, would have to go through that kind of pain and fear ever again. I had no idea at that point how I would do such a thing, but I promised my father and myself that day that I would find another way. The panther had found a voice.

What I didn't know then is that this decision would lead me down a circuitous path not only to study and research, but through dark alleys that, although they seemed at the time like blind endings, actually led me to the door with the key in the lock.

The Music Teacher

In her former life Madelyn had been a music teacher. I say former because her current condition was as far away from that life as the desert is from a lush rainforest. Madelyn had suffered a stroke that had left her paralyzed, partially blind and only able to speak in very short sentences. There wasn't much left in her large frame, and she needed help with everything from bathing to eating. Still, she was always smiling. Everything possessed a childlike joy for her; nothing escaped her attention. Staying in the moment under the burden of what had happened to her would have driven me crazy. For some, it does. Her days were marked off by light and dark, the music of Bach and daytime TV.

She lived in a hospital bed in her living room. Her daily routine consisted of me washing and dressing her, getting her up in a large wheelchair and making a foray into the dining nook of the kitchen to eat breakfast. As with many stroke victims, her left side was paralyzed, but she had some use of her right side. I was awed by her patience.

She had been married to her husband, Terence, for 55 years, he had also been a teacher. Terence was her very best friend and companion, their four boys had long since grown middle-aged and moved away. It was just the two of them now, and there was clearly as much connection now as there had been when they were first married. You could feel it, the bond was permanent.

As for me, after my father died, my life had pretty much gone downhill. Sometimes it's just as well we don't know what the future is, if we did, we wouldn't have the courage to meet it. Any stranger could see where I was headed in two minutes, but of course I couldn't. My marriage had failed mostly from increasingly heavy alcohol abuse, I had been accepted and dropped out of medical school. I had been confronted with the questions that everyone faces, but the answers seemed few and far-between. Some run away from these questions, others stay, many, like Madelyn, don't get a choice.

Even several years after the initial crisis in my life, I was still walking through a maze blindfolded, absolutely nothing made any sense. I had no faith in anything, everything seemed to be a climb up the vertical of a precipice. I had taken a job as a home health aide just to make bills, and that is how Madelyn and I came to meet. She came into my life when the playing field had been reduced to darkened rubble.

I didn't even know what the questions were, but despite my confusion and defensiveness, in the light of her complete helplessness and trust, we became friends. Her quiet but truly happy demeanor was like being out on an early spring morning, not overwhelming in an obvious way, but as pervasive as the sun on bare ground. It was hard physical work to care for her, she was pretty much dead weight when she needed to be moved. But I started looking forward to caring for her each day, which for me was an improvement over the nearly complete darkness in which I was existing. I worked for Terrence and Madelyn for nine months, and I learned many things from her, not the least of which was the true power of the human spirit.

Home health care was not my primary career, neither does it pay very well, so while I had been caring for Madelyn, I had been looking for a job as a laboratory technician. When I got a job in a local hospital and told Terrence and Madelyn I was leaving. They were both sad, but they understood. I felt terrible, but I knew it had to be done. She did not want me to go, and at that moment I didn't want to either. I explained to her that we would always be friends and that I would come visit her often, but the sadness and isolation of these good people was apparent.

The morning I was to start my new job, Terence called me to say that Madelyn had suffered another stroke. I really wasn't surprised, even at this point it was becoming clear to me that there was a link between the mind, the spirit and the physical body. Earlier in my career, I had worked as an emergency medical technician on an ambulance and had seen this too many times to ignore it. It is not unusual to see a spouse follow the other in death very quickly, or serious illness or accident follow a divorce or a job change. Terence told me that she had been admitted to the hospital where I was now employed and was on the medical care floor. There was no blame, we just both intuitively knew why this had happened.

Her sons had been summoned and were present with their father when I went up to see her. Her appearance had changed dramatically, Madelyn was now in a vegetative state. From a smiling woman who had difficulty seeing and spoke slowly, here now was a body whose only evidence of life was from the beep of the EKG monitor. She had undergone a CAT scan earlier in the day and her doctors had reported that her vision and speech centers had been completely destroyed by the tear in her cranial arteries. Her blue eyes, the color of deep summer skies, had always enchanted me, now they were completely opaque. She looked like her own marble tombstone effigy.

Terence was holding her hand by her bedside, speaking to her in a tense, singsong voice about how they would go on a vacation to the Bahamas when she was released from the hospital. Given the charade in which they were trapped, the words rang dully like lead, there was no chance of this woman ever getting back to the point of even speaking her husband's name. Her sons stood around silently or looking out the window, helpless, unable to say anything to their mother or do anything meaningful. The fear that fell down on us like rain had a familiar feel to it. I had felt that fear before, years before, waiting for my father to die.

Madelyn's face was in a severe grimace and she was spasmodically trying to remove the intravenous line that had been installed in her arm. The black, green and purple puncture marks in her arm indicated that she had already been successful a number of times. Terence told me that if she kept tearing them out, that the staff was going to tie her hands to the bedrails, a common procedure. He was trying to convince her to leave them alone, despite the fact that it appeared impossible that she heard him. She was in no physical pain, that had been addressed, but it was clear that she was now suffering.

My new job was occupying my time, so ten days passed before I could go up to see her again, but I wanted a chance to see her alone. I knew she couldn't understand me or even know I was there, but I had to see her. According to Terence, she had not spoken since her stroke. She had mild response to pinprick stimulation, but that was all. She had been moved to a room out of the way by herself, her bed almost against the far wall. When I came in, there was a small pool of light from the lamp next to her bed, making her pale face look like it was cut in stone. The bedclothes were perfect, tucked in tightly around her with mathematical precision. The nursing staff was doing an excellent job, but it was like caring for furniture. Her eyes were half-closed, she seemed more still than death.

Intuitively I knew there was something she needed. I didn't know what it was, but I knew it was why I had come to see her. I wedged myself between the wall and the bed and took a deep breath, my heart was pounding. She was at the end of her life, I was at the beginning, a second beginning, but a beginning. My suffering had been minor compared to hers, I could see that now, if one of us deserved relief, it should be her, not me, I wasn't done yet. I got down head level with hers next to the bed and called her name. I knew she was in there. She stirred slightly and her eyes opened. The words that came out of my mouth literally had a life of their own, I have no idea where they came from, perhaps from the place that recognized another trapped animal. She needed someone to tell her she was free. I took another deep breath and spoke, my voice quavered. But that's part of it, you have to speak the truth to them.

'Madelyn, we love you and we don't want you to suffer anymore. You need not stay if you don't want to. Terence is fine, your children are fine, I am OK, perhaps it's time to let go. I love you, you have taught me so much. I know somehow that I will see you again, but that now is the time to say goodbye.' What happened next will remain with me forever.

'Goodbye,' she replied in a clear, silvery voice, turning her head and focusing her blind eyes on me.

I nearly fainted, the blood in my ears roared. I almost had to crawl out of the room on my hands and knees. I managed to get to a small waiting room and sit there, panting for a while because I couldn't walk. What had just happened? The CAT scan had verified that a major part of her brain had been destroyed by the hemorrhage in her brain, by every definition she was incapable of seeing me or saying anything. But I couldn't deny the fact that the exchange had occurred. There seemed to be a connection between us that I felt physically. It was brief but very powerful, for a moment it felt as if time, space and matter had dissolved. It was just she and I, no human flesh and bone between us, just talking spirit to spirit. I found out later that she died within a half an hour after I left. She had chosen to go home, and me to stay, but that connection between us has never diminished. In doing for her what I could not do for my father, I was also released to go on.

Nightfall

Lessons come in both positive and negative ways. I was still working as a home health care aide when these events occurred, long before I started studying energy work. But I was starting to see some things as being common in the process of transition; while some can transcend the process, others seem to need help. My only regret with Kevin is that I chose not to do more for him. It added to my knowledge about this process, but pointed out in carved relief how much we don't know.

I was still struggling with the uphill climb, many questions that others take for granted were still unanswered. My confidence was still very badly shaken. It really goes even farther than that, when you've used crutches to get through your life, you've got to learn everything all over again, and in some cases, for the first time. But it does have an effect on your perspective when you are faced with a patient like Kevin.

He had been diagnosed with a brain tumor when he was seven years old. I met him when he was nine, he had been assigned to me as a patient. Almost strawberry-blond with blue eyes and an explosion of freckles, he was a handsome child, but cancer had left its mark; he was bloated from steroid use and his head bore scars from several surgeries.

Kevin was a very angry little boy. His biological mother had been in and out of jail for most of his life on a variety of different charges from passing bad checks to dealing drugs. She had finally given Kevin and his younger brother up for adoption, not out of any concern for their welfare, but because she lost interest and told them that she didn't want them anymore. They had been sent out to foster care a number of times, but his temper always prevented them from being adopted permanently. His rages often resulted in much damaged property, he was a big boy for nine years old. There was an issue about which Kevin would tolerate absolutely no compromise; both he and his brother were to be adopted out together, or not at all. His little brother Todd, had accepted most of it with equanimity, at this point in time he seemed to be a fairly normally adjusted 4 year-old.

Kevin's placement became even more complicated when he started having severe headaches again and was diagnosed with another brain tumor shortly thereafter. Surgery had been palliative only, to buy him a little extra time. He had then been treated with radiation therapy, but it seemed to have no effect after the initial course of treatment.

So it was under these circumstances that a young couple, Mike and Beth, adopted the two boys. They had been Kevin's and Todd's last set of foster parents, and despite the fact that they were very aware of both Kevin's condition and his anger issues, Mike and Beth really had fallen in love with the boys, and had taken them in permanently. There wasn't a moment that I spent with them that I wasn't completely awed by these people.

These people were meant to have children. Neither of them were college educated, they both just had a natural ability in parenting. Mike had come from a large Italian family with many siblings; Beth also had a large number of sisters and had been raised on a farm. Initially Beth had been told that she was unable to have children, to their surprise, this turned out to be incorrect. After Kevin and Todd's adoption, Beth became pregnant. They were delighted, and planned to adopt or have more of their own. In a way, what they knew and what they did was simple, they listened, and they were fair. They were the only ones that Kevin really paid any attention to, and in his own stubborn, angry way, loved back.

I worked with Kevin and his parents for three months prior to his death. I use the word "death" because that's what it was. Both of his parents were home most of time, Mike had somehow managed to negotiate afternoons off from work to come and help his wife with the children. I had been hired as Beth had Todd to take care as well as their new son.

Kevin took a lot of care. He had to be supervised for bathing and even playing or walking around, his sense of balance was now affected, and he fell easily. Each CAT scan revealed exactly what they had anticipated, the tumor in his brain was growing rapidly. Eating was always a laborious and unpredictable event, the steroids made it difficult to keep food down, but of course the medication made him very hungry. So despite the fact that he vomited up most of what he ate, an entire bag of cookies could disappear in a minute when your back was turned. Kevin was a very intelligent little boy and wasn't above conning, lying and otherwise tricking those around him into letting him binge on whatever he could get his hands on.

I don't think I ever made much of an impression on Kevin, the gap between himself and other people was just too great. His mother's abandonment had, in a way, broken his spirit. He told me he expected the child welfare agencies to come and pick him up at any time, despite his new parents' constant reassurances that he had a home with them and would never be sent away.

I found it curious that once it seemed Kevin's main objective, making sure his brother had a permanent home had been accomplished, he was now "checking out." Since my own "coming back to the living" and what I had seen with Madelyn, I had become interested in the effect of the human spirit on healing.

I was just starting to see the influence of mental intent on illness, and certainly he was one of the cases that I thought interesting in terms of timing, as in Madelyn's case. He was done, so he was leaving, it seemed as simple as that.

Despite the fact that Kevin really didn't connect with anyone, I quickly became attached to him. He was a very emotional little boy, something I understood. I also understood the feeling of being alone. I was still wary of life in general, despite the things I had learned.

Kevin's passing was not going to be an experience that helped me learn anything positive at the time, either. His illness reignited issues that I had experienced during my parents' passings, the endless medical procedures meant as stop-gap measures only, the waiting, the constant weight of dread. Knowing that you were one day closer to the end, and that today certainly wasn't going to be any better than yesterday. But there was one other issue that had been thrown into the mix. I disagreed with his parents on this point, but he was their child and it was not my decision to make. They had chosen not to tell Kevin that he was dying.

I had wrestled with this, should I tell Kevin or not? Everyone, his parents, all of his doctors, his other caregivers and his teachers all formed a solid block on this issue. They felt that it would be less stressful on Kevin if he didn't know, but he was very bright, surely he had drawn his own conclusions. He had to know this couldn't have a good ending. But this is what they had decided. It caused me much conflict, not really talking about the fact he was dying with my father was one of the things that I thought caused us all so much pain, including my Dad. He had wanted to talk about it. I had been struck mute each time he had tried, I was too afraid, I couldn't do it. I had regretted it ever since. But what could I say to Kevin? What do you say to a nine year-old about his impending death? I had no idea how I felt about this anyway. At this point I was still sort of a nervous agnostic, I was as clueless as anyone else.

Kevin's motor skills were deteriorating rapidly and I knew that time was getting short. We were out for a walk one day in the tree-lined streets around his home, slowly, my arm under his shoulder to steady him. His feet were starting to drag, and walking was slow. We were talking about his little brother. I mentioned that he seemed to be happy.

'Yea, I guess so. Little kids forget stuff.' It was getting difficult to understand him, his speech was starting to slur. A slight breeze ruffled his hair.

'Have you had to forget stuff, Kevin?' I wondered if I could get him to open the door, even a little. I took a breath, and thought, it's now or never.

'I remember everything,' he said flatly. I was sure he did.

'Do you remember your Mom? What do you remember about her?' He shrugged.

'She just couldn't keep us, I guess. It was my fault.'

'What makes you say that?' We were avoiding looking at each other by watching the gold and red leaves drift down from a cement-bound elm in the sidewalk, spent from summer.

'I got mad at her. She told me she didn't want us after that.'

'Well, Kevin, I think maybe there were other reasons. She had taken you back before, hadn't she?'

'Yea. But she kept getting busted.' I remained silent. It was a sad commentary that a nine-year old was familiar with the street slang of the legal system. We watched more leaves fall. He didn't need to feel any worse about the fact that his mother had rejected them. The neglect of a child by a parent is something I do not understand. I took another breath.

'Did anyone ever talk to you about God, Kevin?' I didn't know where else to go with this. He was going to need something to get through the ordeal he was facing, I didn't know what that was, but he needed something. I felt pretty useless, really. I wasn't sure how I felt about God myself.

'Yea, my Mom did.' Well, that was something, although it was probably not from the best source. His freckles were disappearing under a flush of anger, the door was closing.

'And what did you think?'

'There is no God. A real God would not have done this to my brother and me.'

It was the end of the conversation. I couldn't blame him for feeling this way, none of it really made any sense, why the child had to die like this.

Kevin reached a sort of plateau for a few weeks, and because they really couldn't think of what else to do with him, the general consensus was to send him back to school. I found this incomprehensible, if not bizarre. We were in a conference with his teachers, and they were all of the same mind, treat him exactly as the other children were treated, other than that, I would go to school with him to make sure he didn't injure himself. I felt the level of denial by everyone about Kevin's illness was insane. Beth, much younger than the teachers and myself was completely intimidated by the aggressive front they were projecting. I knew they meant well, but enough was enough. I spoke up.

'You know, this really is not taking into consideration what Kevin wants. The child is dying, you know that, don't you?'

Silence. I had said the "D" word. It was as if I hadn't spoken. All of them erupted in talk, loudly, as if to drown out what I had said, a crowd of jays in a cacophony of panicked sound. Beth said nothing.

'Kevin will attend class with his classmates, the same as the other kids.'

'He should be treated as normally as possible.'

'That will cause as little disruption as possible for the other children as well.'

The decision was made as if Beth and I were not in the room. I thought to myself that they would find out soon enough how this was going to work. I think his mother and I were the only ones who really knew how far along the disease had progressed. It was only natural; we were the ones who spent the most time with him.

It didn't take long. Kevin started school the following Monday. At first it seemed like a good idea, he seemed interested and energized in doing something different than staying at home. But he then made it through a half a day and then had to lie down in the nurse's office with a headache. They were nearly constant now. I was fuming as I sat with him. *'For God sakes, stop harassing the child to reassure yourselves,'* I thought. *'Leave him alone.'*

His illness now almost had a palpable form, it lurked in the room like a hungry animal. The heat pulsed off his head, you could feel it keen and roar. Awake and restless, Kevin pulled anxiously at the red blanket he was lying on, his gaze now directed inward. It was now nearly impossible to hold his attention, I just held his hand and said nothing. A half a day of school was all Kevin could stand, that night he had a seizure and he was admitted to the pediatric cancer ward at the local Children's Hospital.

Now began the dark passage that those around the dying person endlessly trudge. For most people, this is a path that is fought against with every ounce of strength we have. I have met hundreds of health care providers that are the walking wounded, they struggle through their jobs completely emotionally depleted.

His parents were with him 24 hours a day, I came up to his room when I could. It didn't really matter though, the only person Kevin could focus on was his father, Mike, and that was only for a moment at a time. He was on a continuous morphine IV pump now and it was the equivalent of giving the child nothing, his level of pain was now obscene. Kevin resembled a moving target on the bed, what parts of him still functioned could not hold still, this was accompanied by a low-pitched howl that stopped only when he paused for breath. In the last week, Mike got no sleep at all, he stayed with him the entire time before his death.

The last time I saw Kevin was two days before his death, he was like an animal that knows he faces the butcher's block. Talking to him about anything was now a moot point, he was too hysterical to listen to anything or anyone. The suffering the child went through was intense. That his parents and the medical staff were doing the best they could for him was never the issue, all that could be done for him was being done. His parents had been there constantly for him, and I knew that it was their own fear and denial as well that prevented them from talking to Kevin about his passing. Who could blame them? I could not. But if there had been any doubt in my mind as to the benefit and even the necessity of at least attempting to discuss this with a person facing that door, there was none now. I carried a lot of guilt for a long time that I was never able to summon up enough courage to talk to Kevin about it.

Yet I had tried and he had resisted, and I feel the patient's wishes must be respected. I do know that his father's presence helped; I don't know how much worse it would have been without him there. Yet I cannot imagine any medieval torture being worse than this.

According to his father, Kevin lost consciousness before he died, small consolation after all that had occurred. After his passing, I gave the family and myself some time to let some of the really painful memories subside before I called them. When I did, I spoke to Mike, I wanted to know where Kevin's burial plot was so I could go visit the site. He told me that he wanted to keep the site private, not even his biological mother knew where he was. I understood, Mike had been deeply wounded by this. What did we all learn? Not much, it appeared, it took me a long time to recover from its darkness and pain. I don't know if it would have helped Kevin at all to try and prepare him for his passing, but anything would have been an improvement over what he and his family went through. With all of our technology, this was no better than an animal dying with its leg caught in a trap. It was clear we had no better understanding of this process than our ancestors did a millennia ago. I didn't know what I was looking for, but my sense of purpose that had been ignited at my father's passing had been refueled, I knew that there had to be something better than this.

Chris and Juni

By now I was starting to get into energy and intuitive work, although rather skeptically, even still. Despite the fact that I have experienced some unusual things with this line of work, I am still essentially trained in the sciences and need to investigate the reasons why things are the way they are. There is a great deal to be gained by observation, even if that's gained in unique ways. Those who have passed over before us are still available to those who listen. Ironically, ours is one of the few cultures that no longer believe this, but it is common to many others. I had experienced a few episodes of mediumship before this, but this was the first interaction I had experienced with someone who had committed suicide, and it was a revelation.

Eventually in my own healing, I ended up doing a great deal of work with drug addicts and alcoholics, and Juni was a young heroin addict who was making an attempt to get clean. Chris had been her boyfriend and partner in drug use for many years.

They met when she was fourteen and he was fifteen in high school. It was one of those instances of "love at first sight" and they were virtually inseparable from the moment they laid eyes on each other. She used to tell me that she felt like only half a person when he was not around and in her case, I don't think she was exaggerating.

Her looks were exotic. Half Phillipino, half Dutch, you couldn't decide if she would look more at home in a gold-embroidered sarong or surrounded by tulips and windmills. With dark hair and delicate features, she would look at home in both, which lent her an air of interesting contradictions. But she was also the quintessential little girl, the last time she got her picture taken with Santa was when she was nineteen, some part of it being a joke, but the most part of her sincerely wishing to remain a child. This got her into no end of trouble, but her extreme intelligence always managed to get her out of it. She was one the few people who could lie to me and get away with it, until I figured her out. But she was also a sweet girl with a "go with the flow" kind of character that made her absolutely charming. Despite not being able to turn your back on her for a second for fear something would turn up missing, she was one of my favorites.

Chris was the son of a lawyer and an engineer, blocky, not at all handsome and nothing extraordinary intellectually, which raised a question of why she had been so attracted to him, but there it was, one of those unexplained connections in life. I never met him when he was alive but I felt I knew him well because their paths were so intertwined. It felt to me like they had some unfinished business from another time, there was no other explanation for the absolute fusion that defined their relationship.

At the height of their drug-using days the two of them together cut a self-destructive swath as wide as a freeway. She would get clean and one phone call from him and she would be using again. Their behavior together was typical of addicts, they lied, they cheated, they stole from each other, their families, their employers, and anyone else naive enough to trust them with anything. Both of them went through drug rehab several times with little effect, compared to the draw of their relationship, it was like spitting on a forest fire. She must have gone back to using heroin at least a dozen times in the time that I knew her. Finally I told her that I would not work with her anymore since nothing we did seemed to have much effect. The last thing I said to her was that this relationship with Chris had to take a break for a while if she were going to make any progress, or even survive.

My hopes for her were very small. There has to be an inner fire, a will to live in there somewhere, and with her I could never see it. She was too placid, too uncaring, as to whether she survived or not. But she finally saw the need to break from the relationship for a while, so she went to San Francisco to go find herself, and to get away from Chris. I felt some hope with this move, but like a parent watching their child climb out on a limb, praying and with my eyes covered. She would either figure it out or fall from the tree. I would occasionally hear from her, and for the most part she was managing to stay clean, or if she went "back out," it would only be for a week or so at a time. But her addictions had changed, now it was anorexia and promiscuity. Her parents were well-meaning but they had problems of their own and were of the same opinion as I was, she was now twenty-four. She was far away and had gotten all the help we could give her, she would have to figure this out on her own.

Chris also had benefited from the separation and had managed to finally get clean. To the delight of everyone he gave the appearance of being the model of sobriety. He started going to 12-Step meetings for his addiction, went back to college, started exercising, and moved in with a mutual friend of both his and Juni's, also in recovery from alcoholism.

Things appeared to be turning around, I was happy for him. Finally the two of them were making some progress! I had always felt the two of them were meant to be together, of course, I had never told them that, they needed to get their lives in order first.

So when Juni called me one Sunday, I was totally unprepared for the news she had to tell me. I had to ask who it was, I didn't recognize her at first, her voice sounded so thin and strangled.

'Chris shot himself,' she said without preamble. I was without words. I had to ask her to repeat herself.

'Excuse me…? What…what happened?' I was stuttering.

'His roommate discovered him Thursday morning. He was sitting in bed, with a bullet hole in his forehead, a gun lying beside him.'

'Juni…Juni, I am so sorry, I had no idea, no intuition about this at all.' I hadn't. I felt guilty, by now I was getting into intuitive work, and it was true, I had gotten no presage, no dream, nothing to tell me he was even thinking about this. Even intuitives get blind-sided.

'Did…did you have any feel for this happening?' I asked her.

'No. I spoke to him on Monday. He seemed busy, he said he could not talk for long, he was studying for a biology exam. Arno called me after the police left.' There were long pauses between her sentences, some nearly inaudible. I had to ask her to repeat herself many times.

'He was just…going through the motions, I guess,' she said. Well, yes, that much was clear.

'Do his parents know yet?'

'Yes, they're going to have him cremated. There's a memorial service on Tuesday.'

'Are you coming back here?' His parents had always disliked her intensely, they considered her too low on the social ladder for their son, I was concerned about how they would treat her.

'Yes, I will be flying in tomorrow. I always thought…that Chris and I would get together again, marry someday. I feel like half of me is…gone.' I had no answer.

Now I was truly in fear for her life. I had done little mediumship work at this point, I was still in training, but I knew I could summon up the energy if I really needed to. This appeared to be one of those times. But there was another issue as well. It takes energy to pass over, much like being born into this life, it's tiring, particularly if one passed over in a violent manner such as a suicide. And in death just as in life, they have free will, they don't have to talk to us if they don't want to. I was hoping and praying that I could get in touch with Chris, and that he would want to talk to her.

I wasn't sure I could do it, but my concern for Juni was outweighing my doubts about my ability. I had to try. I told her what I wanted to do, she agreed. To my relief, Chris came through to me immediately. He stood before me in my living room. I could feel his agitation and distress, he was flickering like a bad TV picture.

'What have you done?' I said as dispassionately as I could. It was too late to berate his choice, if only he had chosen to talk to someone before he did this, but it was done now.

'I made a mistake, I can't believe I did this, I feel really stupid,' he fumed. This was unusual, I have found that usually those on the other side have let go of any unresolved issues in this life and are generally at the very least, resigned to any actions they committed while still alive.

'Why?' I was very interested in this point. All I observed is that he seemed to be creating his own hell, that was all. No fire and brimstone, no one chasing him around with horns and a pitchfork.

'Because now I just have to do this over again. I felt like what I was doing wasn't working, I felt so empty. Now I know it was me that made the mistake. And I left Juni there by herself. If I could do it over again I wouldn't do it.' His energy was becoming even more agitated.

'Well, what's done is done. You can't go back now. Just try and learn what you can from it. Do you have anything for Juni?'

'Yes, tell her I love her and I always will. I will be with her always.' There was a terrible wave of sadness from him, choking me. It was just so sad, regretting killing yourself and having no way to undo it.

'All right. Thank you. Try and forgive yourself, nothing will be served by being angry with yourself for making a mistake.' I felt completely inadequate, but it was all I could think of to say. He did not reply and faded out. He would have to come to a resolution about this on his own.

I turned my focus back to Juni, who had been waiting for me. I told her what he had said, and she finally managed to let a few tears out. I told her how sorry I was, but I doubt that she heard me. There wasn't anything that could make it better, so we hung up.

Many of the Christian traditions believe that suicide immediately consigns that person to hell. The Buddhist traditions tell us that we are immediately "recycled" into the next life, usually with the same lessons to learn. Whether this is true or not I have no more idea than the next person, but it seemed clear from Chris' information that he was just "going to have to do this over again," and that he wasn't being given much choice in the matter. But one thing he still had was his love for Juni, that had transcended even death by his own hand.

Other psychics I have talked to or read have reported similar interactions with those who have committed suicide. Suicide had solved nothing and that they were just going to have to do it over again. There seems to be no way to escape the fact that how we perceive this life is up to us, and to throw it away is meaningless. There appear to be no "Get out of Jail" cards, and "Jail" is all in how we perceive it.

Juni's life descended into a hell that few could have survived. Immediately after Chris' death, his roommate Arno, went back to drinking after nine years of sobriety. Within three months, he died of alcohol poisoning. So in one three month period, Juni attended funerals for two of those whom she had loved most in this life. A heartbreaking experience for anyone to endure, but that is what it took for her to get it. I did not hear from her for a long time, keeping my fingers crossed, hoping and praying, then out of desperation I tracked her down. To my great relief she was doing fine. She had moved away from San Francisco and came back home to the Midwest. She had resumed eating normally and settled down with a new boyfriend. She went back to school and was interning as a social worker. I asked her what had happened. What had caused this complete about-face?

'I realized that everything I do is my choice. And I could do what Chris and Arno did, kill myself, or make my life what I want it to be. It has nothing to do with the past, it's all my choice right now.'

Some people get it, and others don't. There doesn't seem to any predicting who will survive the questions we've been given to answer and who will not. But despite Chris' inexplicable passing and his feeling that it was all so empty, in the long run it did have a point. I hoped that at least he has seen that and allowed it to comfort him. With his passing, he saved Juni's life.

Initiation

This event changed my life forever, my perspective is completely different than it was before this happened. I've told this story many times but I have not written it down before now, it's too intense. People for the most part have a problem with faith, they don't believe something like a Creator or Higher Power or a Unifying Principle is real, and I can't blame them, they've had no proof. We need to see it to believe it. What I came to find out is that there is a "Stream that glorifies the City of God," but you have to ask to be a part of it.

This event occurred when my faith was nearly non-existent. My experiences with Madelyn and Kevin had occurred, but I still had no real idea what to believe. I believed in a Higher Power as a result of being in Alcoholics Anonymous, but not the Catholic God of my childhood, and whoever he was, we weren't on speaking terms anyway. I mention this, because being in AA was, I believe, the foundation of what happened. Thomas Kuhn, a famous sociologist, when asked what was the most significant sociological movement of the 20th century, stated without hesitation, 'Alcoholics Anonymous.' I believe it, I've seen many lives changed by it.

Few people, even those who've never wrestled with an addiction, have missed exposure to AA's 12 Steps, and these have branched into every possible application in addiction and recovery. You can find 12 Step groups focusing on anything from addictions to shopping to sex. Admitting that you are powerless over your addiction and that surrender to a Higher Power is the only thing that can give you the ability to manage your life is the basis of its program. What the Program expressly does not do is permeate the issue with religion. You can, if you wish to do so, but most addicts have been so burned by their religious experience that it's left up to the individual how they want to envision their Higher Power. I used to tell my sponsees—people that you mentor as you gain more sobriety in the program—to start out with the group as their Higher Power.

I never saw anyone make much progress in AA without some form of belief in an outside agency that is available to help.

Even so, success is perilous and hard-won, when it is won at all. I don't have any statistics, but even from my own singular experience, sobriety is hard, and even 25 years out, you can still slip. I suspect that not even 50% make it. But it beats what happened before AA existed. People became drunks, got "wet-brain syndrome"—irreparable brain damage—and then died. No matter what sort of "cures" and sanitariums they were subjected to. That was the harsh reality.

So this story begins in my first year in recovery, and it had been difficult. Yes, I believed in a Creator, but I didn't trust enough to really ask for anything. I never really felt any different after praying and the fear I had lived with for thirty-three years was still very great. As an addict you have to learn how to do everything over again, assuming you knew how to do it before you fell into recovery, and if you were a drunk, then you probably didn't. Fear of everything, of living, of dying, of your past, your future, of just existing from day-to-day, all of it, was what drove you to drink. James Frey got the description exactly right what it feels like to be addicted in his book, "A Million Little Pieces," whatever else he may have made up in the story. It's like having a live animal eating your brain out, slowly, from the inside, until there's nothing left but a locked-eyes view, looking for your next drink.

But in one aspect, I had been very lucky. I had a dog. This dog was the best friend I had ever had. Big, black, with the most expressive eyes I have ever seen on any living being, before or since. He could turn and look at you for a moment with this preternatural stare that was unsettling, they were the eyes of pure wisdom and compassion. He converted dog-haters on a regular basis. When he was with me, the fear was less and the pain receded for a while, to lose him would have been devastating. I remember standing at Detroit Metro after my divorce, thousands of miles away from all that I knew, waiting for our ride. I was petrified, it literally hurt to take a breath, so great was the weight of fear on my chest. We were standing on an island in-between traffic lanes, breathing in jet fumes and exhaust on a humid Michigan day, leaning on each other, and it gave me strength like no other thing. His name was Yiannis, which meant "Beloved

Gift of God." Interesting, as you'll find out later—he came to me with that name.

We had found a place to live on a farm. It was Coplandesque Midwestern tablature, music, not words, described its calm and beauty. It was quiet and the farmers who owned it are still good friends. But it was still a struggle from day-to-day. Everything was brand-new, and not in a good way, panic screamed in a vulgar voice through every single day.

At about a year into recovery, I noticed that Yiannis seemed sluggish. He was sort of middle-aged, only about eight, so this seemed unusual. Always a picky eater, he was now having days of not eating at all. Concerned, I took a closer look at him. I had worked as a veterinary technician, I looked at his gums to check his circulation. In a healthy dog, they're a nice pink color, and the color comes back easily when you press on them. I shrank in fear when I looked at his gums, they were white and had no capillary return at all. He whimpered a little when I pushed him on the side of the chest; this was serious, something was very wrong.

With a terrible sense of impending darkness, I took him to the vet and he agreed, there was a problem, when anemia like this strikes, it's always something very bad. The vet took a chest x-ray, when he came back and showed me the picture, a gaping black hole opened up inside my head and I fell in.

Almost beautiful in its insidiousness, a black butterfly showed on the picture, wrapping around my dog's heart and spreading out through his lungs. It was a tumor, completely inoperable, a Rorschach ink-blot of pain and fear, it looked like a winged demon. The hole burning inside me upon seeing that picture was the worst place I have even been. Even my father's illness had not been this painful. I don't mean that his suffering was less; it's just that my dog had less understanding of why he felt so sick.

The vet said to take him home and make him comfortable; there wasn't much else I could do for him. I could barely walk. I cried and screamed hysterically as I drove home. The only thing that calmed me enough to drive was that Yiannis was visibly upset by my reaction.

Sometimes events are so painful, you'll do anything to get away from them, but this time, I just became insensible. You can't take any more, so you don't. Everything, moving, my divorce, leaving school, it had all become overwhelming. I suppose it's a dissociative technique, we do it to survive. Drinking again was not an issue, getting up, going to work, just putting one foot in front of the other was all I could manage. It would have taken too much focus and energy to even drive to the liquor store. It didn't even occur to me to try.

Nighttime became a period of dread and despair, sleep became impossible. Night was occupied by the utmost blackness, so deep as to possess a sense of malevolent presence. There was an evil feeling—it filled the room, drained the energy out of me. Time wore on like an executioner's sand clock, my dog's physical condition inexorably deteriorated day by day. Getting him to eat anything at all was a constant battle. You'd have thought I had no hope, and that wasn't true. This time was a bit different, perhaps because of my exposure to any sort of help, spiritual or otherwise, in the AA program. I felt there was an answer to this, I just didn't know what it was. It was there in my mind like a pebbled path, every stone I picked up had a tiny nugget of information in it. Underneath the fear, it seemed to be waiting for me to put it all together.

I completely gave up and gave in at this point, but in a different way than to collapse and be overwhelmed by despair. It seemed to be the next step, and I couldn't do anymore than that anyway. My sponsor in AA had given me a booklet on the 46th Psalm. A motivational speaker from the 1920s, Emmett Fox, had written a treatise of how to use "spiritual first-aid," as he called it. He had greatly influenced Bill Wilson in the creation of Alcoholics Anonymous. But the 46th Psalm has a line that has been often quoted, and it stuck with me now, *"Be still and know that I am God."*

So I delivered an ultimatum to whatever was out there listening, if there was anything; either all of this made complete sense, or no sense at all. Why create all this, just to torture your creations? This was either an evolutionary mistake, a waste of energy, or this all meant something. If nothing else, the universe is consistent, that much I knew, it does not waste energy. There couldn't be some parts that made sense and others that didn't. We just don't have all the explanation sometimes. This time I needed an answer.

That night, I laid the gauntlet out on the table. God either had to heal my dog, or take him now, because I didn't see the point of making an innocent animal suffer. Yiannis, at this point, was dying. He was skin and bones, and hadn't eaten anything at all in three days. I stayed up all night in the living room, praying, looking and waiting for an answer and repeating the 46th Psalm over and over again.

Sitting in the living room of this country house, everyone in the house was asleep. Looking across the March stubblefield, as the night went on, the full moon waxed across the sky through the windows. As I went over the Psalm again, sometimes silently, sometimes aloud, something strange started happening. The room, or at least my vision started changing. At first I thought I was imagining it, but then I was sure of it. By 2:00 AM, a thin fog started gathering in the room and began aggregating into patterns. Tall figures started to appear, all moving and weaving in the room. White, with long gowns, that's all I could make out. I could hear small whispers and rustles. I looked down at my dog, asleep on the floor at my feet. I could see a faint, sparkling white stream of energy entering through his head, coursing through his chest, down his body and out his tail. Oddly, I could feel a spark of energy pop in my chest every time I came to the lines of the psalm,

There is a river, the streams thereof shall make glad the city of God,
The holy place of the tabernacles of the Most High
God is in the midst of her
She shall not be moved
God shall help her
And that right early

Being a scientist by training, the first thing that occurs to you is that this is it, you're losing your mind. The stress has become too much, and you're experiencing a psychotic break. Something else was changing as well, I was much less stressed, and felt remarkably more at peace. I thought, well, if this is going crazy, then I'll take it. It felt better than being chased by demons. As night deepened and crept toward morning, the effect was becoming stronger and stronger. By 6:00 AM, the early light starting to streak the sky, I was completely at peace. None of it made any sense, but I felt fine, so I just went with it, and didn't try to fight it. I floated through, trying not to think about anything too hard, to preserve this exquisite quiet I had found.

In the meantime, I had met a woman at the lab where I worked, a crazy cat lady type. She lived way out in the country, even further than I did, with about eighty cats. Seriously eccentric, she was into all sorts of weird stuff, I thought, but she took good care of her cats. At one point I remember her trying to make her cats vegetarian, and they would have none of it. She was a gifted alternative healer, which at the time, I thought was definitely off the beaten track.

She listened with sympathy as I had told her the story of my dog, I even told her that I felt there was an answer, I just couldn't see it. I told her of the events of the night before, she then made an odd suggestion. 'Why don't you come and talk to this friend of mine, she's a psychic. She may be of some help.'

If anyone had suggested this even two weeks prior to this happening, I would have said they were crazy. This was not aligned with how I looked at life. I had been raised Catholic and then influenced by strict Christianity, and then trained as a scientist. Such things were highly discouraged in all of these areas. But this time, as I said, I was completely overwhelmed and open to new ways to see things.

I told her, 'Fine, why not?' Nothing else had helped or worked, and as with my father, conventional medicine had nothing to offer my dog at this point. The psychic's home was deep in the backcountry of Michigan, it took us over an hour to get there. I was a bit concerned about the impending experience, but mostly just very curious. Was she going to be a complete basket case? A dark-looking woman wearing a headscarf? If she whipped out a crystal ball, or even saw one in her house, I swore I was going to run out the door.

She was none of those things. She looked like your grandmother. I think she was actually baking cookies. Of course I found out later that she knew alarming me in any way would result in me running, but she really was about as intimidating as a teddy bear.

Tina Marie had been a practicing psychic for 40 years. Grey now, she had been strawberry-blond with glacial blue eyes, and in her heyday a great beauty. I believed it, I could see it, she was still striking. But what was most compelling about her was her gentle yet pragmatic manner. Very down-to earth, no nonsense, but very kind.

I don't remember much of the reading. She said I would write, which I found hard to believe at the time. I was so pre-occupied that I really didn't pay much attention. But at the end of it, she asked me if I had any questions for her.

'Yes,' I said, struggling for the words. 'My dog is sick, and I know that there is something else out there for him. I am a scientist by training, and there is nothing in conventional medicine that can really help him. Yet I know—and it doesn't make any sense—that there is something out there that can help him.' My voice quavered, I felt the key hidden somewhere nearby.

'Well, dear,' she said with a smile, 'Why don't you do what you did when you were working on the ambulance?' First of all, she couldn't possibly know what I did years ago working on the ambulance in LA because I hadn't told her. But it bears on the story, so allow me to take a side path for a moment.

Many years ago, I had worked as an emergency medical technician in the LA area. There was plenty of opportunity to see a lot of action, it was an eye-opener. Mostly car accidents, or MVAs as they're known in the trade. GSWs, (gun-shot wounds) sick person down, FUBARed patients (very badly injured), Frequent Flyers (just like it sounds-you picked them up frequently for any number of causes), domestic disturbance (a couple fighting—often involving guns—a life-threatening situation), we saw it all.

As an EMT at that time, you had little chance to do anything significant to help your patients. You couldn't call for a code or give medication, so your only option was do what was called "scoop and run." It was pretty much what it sounds like, you collected the patient and whatever pieces you could find, and drove like a bat out of hell to the ER, hoping that you would make it in time.

Some of these patients were badly injured, so much so that you wondered what could be done for them. It left me feeling pretty frustrated. So I developed a technique of just holding their hand, or whatever exposed part I could find and just thinking love at them. So here's where it gets weird.

Those people that I managed to do this with actually got better. Sometimes a lot better, when they shouldn't have. Of course, the first thing you think of is that it couldn't possibly be happening, that it's just a figment of your imagination. But it kept happening. This went on for some time, it occurred to me to try and ask someone about it, but there was no one who could possibly have any advice or even had any experience with it. Who would I ask, the ER personnel? I'd be laughed out of my job. So I dropped it, and after I left, I pretty much forgot about it.

So now we come back to an old lady telling me that I should to the same thing for my dying dog, years later and many miles away. Again, I thought, that's it, I have officially gone past the lines of sanity and now I need help. But when I looked at it pragmatically, I had no other options available. My dog would be dead in days, and this would not hurt him. I thought she was mad, but so was I, so I listened.

'Go home and put your hands on him and ask him to be perfect. Imagine the energy running through him like you saw the other night. Don't visualize the problem; see it as flawless and already done. Give thanks when you are done— this is very important.'

I went home in a dream-state, but I was also curious. Something had happened with all those people years ago, could I repeat it? I had no idea and felt nervous about trying. Did I deserve a gift this great? Was it even possible? I tried to avoid thinking about it and maintain that sense of peace I had garnered from my night of repeating the 46th Psalm.

I had to work that day at 3:00 PM, so I tried it on him as soon as I got home. The situation was desperate, he hadn't eaten in days at that point. But I was still at peace. From what I learned later was that this sense of "The job is already done," is critical to this technique working. I leaned over him and putting my hand on his head and the other hand on his back, I visualized him as being healed. I stayed like that for about 15 minutes, my hands getting hot and pulsing like they did so many years ago.

I left for work and tried not to think about anything too hard. My shift passed slowly, I didn't know how I felt about going home. I drove home in a trance. When I parked in the garage, I sat in the car for at least 15 minutes, I didn't know what I was going to face, a dead dog or a live dog, I didn't know if I could face either one. Finally, I was forced out of the car, it was early March in Michigan, and I was getting cold.

When I opened the door, my dog was standing there wagging his tail. The dog whom eight hours earlier couldn't stand up, was bounding around, wanting to go outside. I opened the back door and let him out, he ran out and immediately lifted his leg on a tree. He then ran off, jumping and playing in sheer joy.

The inside of my head hurt, my ears rang. I had looked at his food bowl, he had eaten three pounds of cold cuts that I had left for him. As I watched him run, a bag of bones, still, everything I knew inside my head about healing and medicine was yanked out by the roots and set aside. Not thrown out, just moved over. Not only that, but my entire life view changed in an instant.

I had no words, inside or out. As I walked around the yard, there was a light in everything, all seemed illuminated. The edges of the leaves of the early spring, the shoots of the flowers, the grass, all was alive. I heard a buzzing in the yard, another presence; a voice in my heart said,

'This is what I will do for you if you ask, but you must ask.'

I went back the veterinarian, who confirmed that my dog had been healed. I told him what happened, he stated he had no explanation for what had occurred. I went back to the psychic, she smiled and said,

'Of course, dear, I knew you could do it. This happened so you could learn how to do this.'

But the thing that struck me was that nothing I had done up to that point had earned me such a gift. With all of my stupid mistakes, I had earned no "brownie points," I had been given this tremendous thing just as a result of my asking. What more could any of us do, if such a thing were available to us, just for the asking?

This began the journey of a lifetime, of inquiry and of faith. My dog lived for another five years, long enough for me to get better and find my balance again. He certainly lived up to his name, "Beloved Gift of God," for so he was.

The White Tiger

After the blunt revelation the epiphany my dog's healing had led me to, I went back to the psychic and apprenticed to her for two years, eager to study first-hand the interaction between divine and human will to bring about healing. It seemed clear that there is an ever-moving dance between intention, faith, wisdom and creativity that determines our path here. But learning how to do this, to lead people to their healing brings about many lessons. And the first and ever-present one, the Prime Directive, so to speak, is when to know to let them go, your will is not their will. This is a tough one.

I was well into my work as a Reiki practitioner by now and was beginning to work extensively with patients with cancer. In the US we most commonly know it as "faith-healing," and it certainly has acquired a suspicious reputation as such, with images of itinerant preachers with snake-oil tendencies yelling at crowds and throwing people to the floor coming to mind. But in other cultures it has a very long history and is an essential part of their healing system. Some of the names by which it is known are Reiki, Therapeutic Touch, Polarity Therapy and Qi Gong, although these are by no means all of them. Many people in the US use them in conjunction with their conventional Western treatments and the number grows every year. In the UK it's even more common, with conventional medical practitioners recommending it as often as not.

The basic idea behind it is that we all have an energy field that can be altered by another person trained to identify these energy fields and correct deficits in it. It's something we all do, consciously or not, and is actually easy to learn. But I have to come to find out that it has a much simpler name, the Beatles got it right, all you need is love.

Tom was 45 when he was diagnosed with kidney cancer. This is a particularly aggressive form of cancer and is usually dealt with swiftly with surgery combined with radiation treatment. From a neurological perspective, the kidneys are so close to the spine, that in reality, it's an easy jump to the brain, so often, that's what happens. When I met him he now had a brain tumor, and the affected kidney had already been removed. He had subsequently gone through several rounds of radiation treatments, none of which had been successful. When I met him and his wife, Susanna, it was in the middle of a brief respite from treatment and surgery. It was clear from the progressing CAT scans that the outlook was grim, but no one talked about it.

Tom's wife, Susanna, whom I had worked with at the hospital on my "day job" in the laboratory, had approached me about working on her husband. Her fragile hope touched me, but it was really against my better judgment. Frequently it is the relative's agenda one is confronted with when approached by someone other than the patient, and one has to be clear whom this is really for, or it won't work. But after speaking to Tom and explaining how I worked, he appeared willing to try it with me. We both knew why, even at the beginning. It was for Susanna.

Tom was a rather quiet man, balding, with steel gray hair and the most amazing glacier-blue eyes. They were like wells of memory going back a million years and not just for his lifetime, it was like race-memory, knowledge from the collective unconscious. They would have been disconcerting had they not been softened by a warmth and a natural affection for everyone. He was one of those people who had the ability to ask you the right question about your life at the right time. Never judgmental, always accepting, he just had a knack for pointing out the door that you hadn't seen. He worked as an air-conditioning maintenance technician at the same hospital that his wife and I worked. He had great mobility throughout the hospital, so all of the staff from the interns to the head of the hospital knew him, and had the utmost respect for him. He could show up at the right moment with those ageless eyes and quietly ask you the most amazing questions. In his own quiet way he had changed just about everyone's lives by some penetrating comment he made to them about a life passage they were facing. No one who knew him were left untouched. Tom was a healer.

But the first time I worked on him, a very odd thing occurred. Something I have learned is that the patient must agree on a very deep level to allow healing to happen. We were sitting on the porch in their backyard, it was lovely, both of them were talented gardeners. Their garden had a peculiar quality to it, all of their flowers and shrubs had a very alive feeling to them. It was high summer in the Midwest, a beautiful season anywhere but there it exudes such a feeling of growth that it seems like a barely controlled explosion.

But despite the beauty of their garden, an unspoken pall was over them both, almost like another entity present with us, his voracious cancer. Susanna was clearly suffering the most. All of the treatment options had been tried, and it appeared that none of them were working to stop the growth of cancer in her husband's brain. It was now affecting his memory and motor skills. The slow loss of her husband before her eyes is a cruelty that people whose loved ones are dying of Alzheimer's as well as brain cancers know, it is a unique pain that defies description. They're there, but they're not, they move farther away from you every day, and you are helpless to stop it.

Susanna was an intelligent, quiet woman with a pleasant demeanor who probably would have stayed single for her whole life had she not met Tom. The story of their first date had sent me into gales of laughter when Susanna told it to me. Tom had been no great shakes as a lady's man, as a matter of fact, he had rarely dated at all. On their first night out he was very nervous, so he drank to settle his nerves, with the predictable result. He got absolutely smashed, not being much of a drinker either. She had to drive him home and pour him out of her car onto his doorstep. In spite of this terrible first impression, she really liked him and she knew it had been because he was nervous, but she felt unable to approach him again to let him know. But it was Tom who saved the day. He had the presence of mind and the humility to call her to apologize and ask if they could just start over. They married three months later, knowing somehow that there was no time to lose, and it was a perfect match. The two of them together possessed only one frequency, one would start a sentence and the other would finish it. Their families got along perfectly. They liked the same things, drove the same model cars, which were even the same color. They both functioned perfectly well separately and yet were one unit when they were together. When I had met them, they had been married for 17 years.

We spoke for a while within the oasis of an eternal summer day. Tom was having difficulty getting up on a treatment table at this point, so I worked on him while he was sitting in a lawn chair. But as I put my hands on his shoulders, as I said, something odd happened. With energy work, if the person you are working on has not given you permission to help them, the energy will not flow between you. I noticed that immediately beginning to work on Tom, I could feel the energy bouncing back at me. I said nothing aloud, but asked him silently whether he wanted me to do this. You hear the answer in your heart.

'*No, I do not want to heal my physical body, I am leaving,*' he said.

'*Oh. All right. Can you take the energy for something else? Perhaps to relieve your pain? That would not change what you need to do, would it?*'

'*Yes, that would be OK,*' I heard him say. I could feel the energy immediately start to flow into his shoulders. I finished the session and said nothing to either of them about what I had perceived.

I always have a lot of difficulty letting go of the people I work on. I still do, to this day. I believe most health care providers are like this, and it really doesn't get any easier as time goes on. You get attached to them, it's unavoidable. I don't think you can be compassionate without it. But it was Tom who showed me how to do it, or at least how to begin.

That night I had a vision within a dream. This one was brief and powerful. In the early hours of the morning, a voice shouted at me so loudly I nearly fell out of bed, it scared me half to death. A magnificent white Siberian Tiger reclining in a jungle clearing sat before me; his paws extended out gracefully in front of him, crossed, his glacier-blue eyes serene and detached. I recognized the eyes immediately, it was Tom.

'*The Spirit of the White Tiger has gone home. Let go.*' a voice said.

I didn't get much more sleep that night. I thought long and hard about what had been said to me. It seemed clear to me that Tom had fulfilled what he had come here to do and was preparing to leave.

At this point in my training, this just caused me more anxiety. What should I tell them? Sometimes in this line of work you get information you feel that should not be passed on. The future is always changing, what if you are wrong?

For a week I virtually got no sleep at all. It was clear that Susanna was hoping for healing for Tom, but he was in a very accepting space about where he was. It also seemed clear to me that he was waiting to help ease her fear of his impending transition.

It became apparent to me that on a very deep level this is what he wanted, it was time to for him to go. In the end this is what made my decision. I was there for Susannah, not Tom. But when the issue came up, what would I say to her? Finally I decided to tell her exactly what I had seen, with the caveat that I could be wrong.

I asked her to lunch at a local coffeehouse. When I recounted my vision to her exactly as I had seen it, I then asked her what conclusion she would come to. We were silent for a moment. Tears welled up in her eyes and she said almost inaudibly,

'I know. I think I have always known. When he had his last recurrence, when it reappeared in his brain, we discussed long and hard whether it would be worth it to have it removed. It had already been decided that the whole tumor could not be removed without damaging his brain significantly. But in the end we decided that it would buy him a little more time. But a strange thing happened, the imaging instrument the surgeon was using broke down right before the surgery, Tom was already anesthetized and the entire surgical team was waiting for the instrument to come online. I knew at that point that this wasn't meant to be. We ended up leaving it where it was.'

'And what did Tom think about this?' Perhaps Tom himself had the answer to this question for her.

'We didn't talk about it much, but he seemed to accept it, even with some relief.'

'It must be very hard for him to go through this, perhaps we need to honor what he needs to do in this situation.'

'I know. But it's so hard, I can't even imagine, I don't *want* to imagine what it would be like without him there.'

'Yes. We miss them physically so much when they are gone. But as much as we can, I think we need to adhere to what they want and how they want to transition. But the best I think we can do is a minute at a time sometimes. This seems to be one of those times.'

'But why, why *now*? He's only 47! This is just not fair! How could he want to leave without me?' Her tears started again. I had screamed this question late at night myself to what seemed to be nothing and had gotten no answer.

We never spoke of it again. We continued to work together for another three months but Tom continued to deteriorate slowly. He was admitted to the hospital when his motor skills got to the point of his not being able to take care of himself. His memory was now sketchy, there were times when he did not remember visitors, although he always remembered Susanna and me.

I went to see him the day before he left here, he was on heavy doses of morphine, but I could see that his energy field, a smoky haze around him, was becoming looser and that his relatives in spirit were gathering in the room. I could see their outlines. By now I had advanced to the point of being able to see people in spirit. The gathering relatives in spirit of the person preparing to transition is always a sure sign that it is impending. Soon, I thought. Whispers and rustles surrounded us.

He had not really been speaking or even aware of anyone, but he immediately sharpened and came back when I entered the room. Now's the time to talk about it, I thought. But I had to be careful, he was still in massive denial himself. I had asked Susannah and his family to give us a few minutes alone. I drew up a chair and settled next to the bed.

Conversations with the dying are often stilted, so don't blame yourself when yours are the same. We do the best we can.

'So Tom, how does this all look to you? What do you think is happening?' I said without much preamble. I could feel the door crack open a little.

'Not so good,' he said slowly. His speech was slurred but he was here with me, a good sign. He had been sliding in and out of consciousness for a day or so and had spoken to no one except his wife.

'We have worked hard, haven't we? It's OK, I have no vested interest in whether you stay or whether you go. It's truly all the same to me. But can I tell you what I have observed when others have passed? Is this something you might like to know?'

He said nothing, but his eyes said yes. I told him what I had seen in the past with others, that it was merely passing from one frequency to the next. By now I had witnessed a number of people pass, and it had been a fascinating process from an energetic point of view. In all cases I had seen that it had never been an isolated chain of events, all their relatives already in spirit had been there to greet them, every time. He wouldn't really be leaving here from his point of view, only from ours. I asked him if he was afraid, but I already knew the answer.

'No.' The door flew wide open for a moment; it was just the two of us.

'Why have you fought this so hard? It seems to me that you are ready to go.'

'For Susanna. She can't handle it.'

Without knocking a nurse entered the room with fresh linens, I wanted to scream. It had taken months to get to this point. The door slammed shut.

'I know. That's all right. But she can handle it better than you think. You must do what you need to do for yourself now. It's all right if you let go. You have been such a guiding light for so many people, including me.'

There was no answer. I looked into his face, he had faded out again.

Tom passed away the next day surrounded by his family. He fought it tooth and nail to the end and so therefore it was not pleasant but since they made no attempt to resuscitate, it was relatively peaceful.

Much later I told Susanna the last words Tom and I had exchanged. I did not want her to feel that somehow that her inability to let go had prolonged his suffering. He had chosen to stay and fight it.

'You know that we all do what we need to do, he stayed because he wanted to.' I wanted to make sure she understood this point.

'Yes, I know that now. But I just couldn't let go, even now it's hard to realize he's gone.' She looked at me sadly, but I could see that part of this guilt had lifted.

'It's so hard to let them go. We just don't know if we will ever see them again, and really, we just want them back. But it's the ambiguity that's so difficult to accept. We just have to wait and see. But I do know that love is indestructible, it transcends everything, even death. You will remember him, and if there is some part of him that is eternal, and I believe that there is, then he will remember you. You are a part of who he is. That is forever.'

It seemed clear that we have more choice about when we pass than most people realize. Some stay out of fear, some stay for unfinished business, some leave because they chose to do so. Some stay for love, even when they know they are leaving.

Another question plagued me as well. Who was Tom? Why had he only been here for 47 years? According to most standards, he hadn't possessed much, nor had he made much of a mark on the world, he hadn't been a Rockefeller, or a Jobs. But he had left a legacy, nearly 400 people attended his memorial service including the director of the hospital, he had affected all of them in some way. His effects may have been small, but they will not be easily forgotten. But one thing he showed me was to be mindful of how you treat small and the meek, for they may be angels in disguise.

Second Wind

Another lesson that proved critical to my understanding of the dying process comes from the story of Regina. It was also one of the hardest to tell simply because words do not meet the task. Death, a process we must all go through, is also a process we have more control over than we can possibly imagine. It takes unblinking courage to walk into the unknown, unafraid, but it can be done.

Regina was an extraordinary woman. I had seen a photo of Regina and her husband, Alan, that really typified the energy they shared. Taken at a family picnic, the picture showed Alan leaning into her shoulder as the two exchanged some confidence. She was like a Nordic beauty queen, a beautiful blond with blue eyes, and in this picture she looked like the Sun that Alan and their children revolved around. She was clearly the queen of her household.

She was despotic in some ways, but she ruled her family, really everyone within her sphere of influence, with love and guardianship. For twenty years she cooked for a grammar school, making lunches for the children. She was not a chef, nor would she have called herself one, but she put caring into everything she made. Her realm was created with bonds of love and loyalty.

At the age of 42, Regina was diagnosed with breast cancer. She went through two bouts of chemotherapy and a mastectomy to treat it, but these measures were not completely successful. They had given her a respite of fourteen years, but when I met her, a CAT scan had just revealed the appearance of spots on her liver. No one spoke of it directly, but everyone knew what that meant: the cancer was back.

There are often many unspoken hierarchies and imperatives in a family; to Regina, this meant a lifetime spent as the dominating caretaker. But after working with her for a few sessions, I perceived on a deeper level that Regina had now decided that there were other things she wanted to do, and that it was time for her family to take responsibility for themselves. As is true of many families, not being able to tell them directly, her leaving was the easier way.

There is a point here that needs to be made very clear; this is not something that a patient decides on a conscious level, neither is it their "fault" when this choice is made. I have seen this over and over again from the ambulance to the bedside. Sometimes the disease is something that we agreed to experience to learn something about living this life, sometimes it seems to be because of some emotional or spiritual need that cannot be articulated, but that at some level and at some point, the choice to leave is made.

We immediately attach all sorts of value judgments to this subconscious process because we are so terrified of dying. That this is wrong or crazy in basis, that we're blaming the patient, no one could make a decision on this level, how could I accuse someone of leaving the people they love behind? I think that perhaps where our eternal self, our soul lives, we understand a great deal more than we consciously are willing to accept. Humans are designed for survival, and in the face of a contradiction in this life that we cannot correct, deny or accept, we choose a way out of the situation, knowing that survival will continue elsewhere. To those of us here, though, it's a seeming paradox. This paradox can present contradictions to the person leaving that are difficult for their loved ones to accept. When I recognize that someone has come to that juncture, my task as a healer is not only to respect the decision, but also to define the process as a natural one, to be clear that death doesn't have to be frightening or painful.

Even though Regina recognized a Higher Being and an afterlife intellectually, she, like the rest of us, really didn't know what lay before her. So we worked feverishly together for a physical healing for nine months; no one could accuse either of us of slacking on the job. But the slow progression of her disease became more apparent with each passing week.

Regina's perspective as a caretaker had been shaped by events that had occurred in her childhood. When we think about this from a rational perspective, it's almost funny how as adults, many of us are still allowing a memory from half a century ago to drive the way we think about our role in this life now.

When she was six years old, her mother died. Children always take a parent's death personally, they can't help it. For them, the emotional maturity to look at it any other way doesn't yet exist. The concept of "It has no reason, it just is," is not an idea they are capable of wrapping their head around. It's hard enough when we're adults, isn't it? All she knew is that her mother had left. Regina had taken this to mean that she was somehow responsible for her mother's leaving, and she took it to heart.

Another event occurred that crystallized Regina's perception of herself as caregiver, when she was ten years old, her father remarried. Soon after their marriage, her new stepmother took Regina and her two sisters aside and told them that her own children were more important, that they could count on nothing but the bare necessities from their father and that they were to move out of the house when they were eighteen. They were on their own.

In my experience, children need a connection with an adult caregiver to establish their own identity and a sense of personal value. Those who do not, spend the rest of their lives looking for it in the relationships and experiences we pursue.

This also can deeply affect our physical health. For Regina, this was a betrayal in the deepest sense of the word, and she never forgot it. As it is becoming clearer that our health and wellbeing are deeply integrated, it is interesting that of the three siblings, two passed at less than sixty years old of breast cancer. In energy medicine, the heart chakra is the province of self-love. When there is a weakness or blockage in that area, physical illness can manifest in that area of the physical body.

While we were working together, about two months before her passing, Regina had a dream. She was dancing on a stage with her sister who had already died, her family was in the audience. The bare stage and the audience were dark except for a spotlight, which was focused on the dancers. They were wearing beautiful ball dresses, but the music was frenetic and out of control. Regina was feeling exhausted and struggling to keep up.

'I'm tired, I don't want to do this anymore,' she said to her sister.

'So stop,' her sister replied, dancing around her, their arms joined together. There were cries of 'No, don't!' from her family in the audience. There the dream ended. The meaning seemed clear, but on the conscious level, neither

Regina nor her family was ready to accept this. Neither was I, as I said, even healers get attached to outcomes. I had no comment, we ignored it and plowed on, but I couldn't get it out of my mind.

A short time after this dream occurred, she experienced a brief improvement, a second wind, from which her relatives took great hope, but I have seen this before. Often before someone passes there is a respite so that the person can settle accounts, so to speak, loose ends can be tied up, good-byes can be said. She told me that she wanted to go to Hawaii where her son was stationed while in the Marine Corps. She had not seen him in two years and dearly wished to visit him. She was now in a wheelchair but could function well enough, so I suggested that she go. They had a wonderful time, but I knew a decline was coming once she returned, particularly with the dream constantly lurking in my thoughts. Though she had been retaining fluid in her belly from a blockage in her tormented liver, it had been remained fairly static for a long time. On her arrival home it immediately became more aggressive, now distorting her appearance; the whites of her eyes were becoming yellow. This was it, the dying process was beginning.

Again the argument within myself about how much to tell her rose its tormenting head, how much I was willing to face myself. We had fought tenaciously for so long to give her what she wanted! I had grown to love her and selfishly did not wish her to pass, not just yet. I saw this later as a mistake but also came to realize that synchronicity operates at levels we don't understand at the time.

It was now becoming clear that we had to let her go, despite her family's opposition. The family's terrible grief and fear often influence the patient to stay, but at great cost, these ties are strong, but Regina was still leaving. Her body experienced a frightening and humiliating decline, as the medical measures used to keep it here were invasive and painful.

One snowy afternoon at the end of January, I asked her what direction she thought she was going. It was becoming clear that matters were coming to a head; Regina's skin was now becoming yellow and her belly was grotesquely distended in a travesty of new life, she looked nine months pregnant. We were alone in her living room.

'I don't know, but it doesn't look good,' she said, looking frightened and demoralized.

'That depends on your point of view,' I replied. 'We have worked hard, haven't we?'

We had been to the ends of the earth together; we had already talked about everything, so no more could be said, not right now, anyway.

'Well, I'm not leaving right now,' she said.

'No, it isn't today,' I affirmed.

A long silence followed. We knew it was coming.

The call came less than a week later about 10:00 PM on a Sunday night. Her husband, Alan, called and told me with a shaking voice that it was time to come now. Her sister and her husband were in the living room when I arrived, they were near hysterics. It was one of those horrible moments when everyone knows what is happening and no one can stop it. They were hoping for a miracle, we were going to get one that none of us could possibly imagine.

I spoke to them briefly, but they didn't hear me. Anything I could have said would have sounded like a platitude anyway. I moved down the darkened hall to Regina's room. We all have so much terror about this process.

Regina was lying on a couch with an adjustable back and footrest to be more comfortable. She was not on pain medication; she said she didn't need it. Hospice had been contacted a few days before and they had made the offer of pain control at home with a morphine pump, but she had refused it. She had no fear, so her pain and discomfort were greatly reduced. I have come to find this out, that addressing the anxiety can be as powerful as administering a narcotic and allows much more presence of mind. But then Regina was exceptional. She told me that she didn't want anything because she didn't want to miss anything. She was an amazing woman.

The light was low in the room, so I could now see her energy field easily. It was finally loosening, it looked like an old sock, gaps were developing between her body and the vague circle around her, now sort of a smoky grey. One can see these things with some practice, and this was always a sure sign that her leave-taking was beginning. The corners of the room were moving with shades and murmurs. Her family was gathering to greet her in spirit, I could see and feel them. Her look was far away, but she came back when I entered the room. She smiled at me peacefully.

Suddenly it snapped into focus for me, I felt both of us standing on the edge of a cliff of understanding. We joined hands and looked over the edge. There was nothing there and yet it was totally comfortable and familiar. It was still life. Nothing frightening, no oblivion, nothing like that, it was just the next step. How ridiculous all this fuss had been, we spend our whole lives refuting this, denying it, centering our whole culture around its existence, and it's nothing. It was like being in your house, and leaving one room and entering another.

'How are you doing?' I asked with a smile. It was just the two of us, no one else could go where we were going.

'Fine. I can't really get into a comfortable position, but I'm OK.' She shifted around again, feeling for a better spot. She was wearing a beautiful scarf on her denuded head, I smiled at her consciousness about her appearance. I smiled, she wanted to look good crossing over. That was Regina for you.

'We have worked hard, but this is it. Are you scared?' We both understood the question to be so silly that we both laughed. There was nothing to be afraid of. Later Alan asked us what could we possibly have been laughing about in the face of death. I couldn't really explain it to him at the time, the change in perspective had been so profound.

'No.'

'Your sister and mother are waiting for you. Love is all there is.'

'I know.' We smiled at each other.

'Do you want me to stay?'

'No, it's alright. You go.' She shifted again on the couch.

'They're pretty upset out there.' We could both feel the tension in the other room. She smiled in an annoyed way.

'This is no big deal.'

'True,' we both laughed again, looking down at the pit that wasn't there.

'You will not be alone. I love you, Regina.'

'I know. I love you, too.' We hugged for a long time. I had tears in my eyes, her healing, the one she had wanted, was very close. Not the one we had worked for, but one of far more permanence and power. Her family in spirit crowded around, waiting for her, relaxed and joyous.

Regina passed out of her body at 6:00 AM the next morning. Alan called me and told me.

'Are you OK?' I asked him. He was in awe; somehow he had gotten it.

'Yes, it was…amazing. There was no fear, no pain, she just…slipped out. I've never seen anything like it.'

We think that we walk through the door alone, but nothing could be farther from the truth. I had witnessed many people pass, but never had either of us witnessed the way it should be, with all our eyes open. Death has no meaning, other than to tell us that in our family, in the family of humankind, love is all there is.

Sarah

This episode was the culmination of much study, meditation and focus, but probably also the result of a lot of dumb luck as well. No less than a doctoral level class in the process of dying, it represented a breakthrough that left me completely different than I was before. Any residual fear I had after Regina's passing, the difference between "here," the living, and "there," the dead, lost meaning for me as the result of this experience.

Visions were becoming more and more frequent at this point, with more evolved levels of information in them, so I suppose I should explain the nature of a vision. Fair warning: if this makes you uncomfortable, then think of it as an allegory. There is much to learn from that perspective as well, for what happened to Sarah is really the story of all of us at one point or another.

My experiences have taught me that all possible worlds are an overlay of this one. Current Universal Field Theory is actually dancing around with these concepts, while those of us who work with these different levels of consciousness have known about these different "layers" for a very long time. From my perspective, your relatives who have gone on before you are as close to you as a thought. Granted, it would be nicer if they were physically here with you, but from what I have observed, the important part of them is right here with you, right now. They love you, where else would they be?

These different levels of awareness are like watching television. You may be watching channel XYZ, but you are aware that Channel QRS is also on right now, showing a different program. This particular reality happens to be the one we are all watching right now, but there are other channels; it's as simple as that.

I am not going to make up rules about who or what lives in each one. Those seem to differ with the intuitive person, and I suspect, dovetail in many respects with what we want to see to some degree. I am unlikely to visualize the Peaceful and Wrathful Deities of the bardos of Buddhism, part of their death process.

Based on my experience though, if I did see them, I would understand that they represented some underlying truth, and not a set of real demons or angels.

Neither have I in all my travels actually seen visions of heaven or hell, nor have any of the people that I have talked to in spirit. I have run into spirits who were pretty darned surprised to be there, and others who were regretful, such as Chris, but whatever seems to be "here," seems to be "there" as well, it just seems that the level of perception and knowledge is different. This isn't to say that we can't project places and things that are pretty awful, as you will see in the case of Sarah.

None of this is set in stone; as such, it can be corrected—according to your perception. In other words, it is never too late, even after loved ones have passed, to help them improve their situation. A visit with spirits, as near as I can tell, is when your brain, the conduit, has "accelerated," your perception, allowing your TV set to pick more channels, while those in spirit have slowed theirs down, so that an intersection is possible.

Sometimes it's more like stepping into TV Land for a moment and then backing out, leaving those in that channel behind. How do you know it's real? You don't. But after doing it a number of times and getting information that is verifiable in this reality, then you come to know when it's real and when it isn't. But you have to be careful, it can be tricky and overlaid with your own desires and cultural perceptions. It's probably the reason why different psychics get different details in messages about the same topic, although if they're good psychics then there are usually commonly identifiable themes.

Sarah was a young woman that I never met in this life. I worked with her sister-in-law, Lauren, in my day job in research. She was militantly atheist as was her entire family; Lauren was the most linear thinker I had ever met. She had her Master's degree in biology and statistics, if there was no evidence, to her way of thinking, it simply did not exist. She could not even debate the point, her only response to a comment within this arena was a quizzical stare and silence. However, confronted with Sarah's impending death, she finally asked me for help. I knew her family had to be desperate at this point, their viewpoint on reality and mine possessed no intersection point. Although I did not advertise it, it was well known that I worked with patients with cancer and had met with some success using Reiki and meditation.

Sarah was being treated for non-Hodgkin's lymphoma, an aggressive form of lymphatic cancer. She was twenty-one years old. She had gone through three courses of chemotherapy, yet no treatment was successful in preventing her body from eating itself alive. She and her family had fought it with terrified ferocity for three years, but she was now approaching the end stage. When faced with Lauren's desperation and fear, I could not say no, but as I have said, I am hesitant to work on a relative when it's the family member who has asked me. The patient must want it, no one else, or it won't work. I told her that I would help her, but that I had to hear it specifically from Sarah.

I heard no more for about three weeks. I knew Sarah's condition was very serious and that she was in the hospital requiring palliative care, the pressure was coming to a critical point. It had been a terrible fight, but they were facing the end.

During a meditation one Sunday afternoon, a commanding voice yelled at me, "SARAH," so loudly it yanked me upright and nearly threw me off my seat. It always scares me half to death when this happens, it really gets your attention. Recovering, I replied, 'Yes, what is it? Can I help you?'

Instantly I was pulled into another place, a hospital bedside where a tiny skeletal figure, a young woman, was taking her last breathes. The rattle of her breath filled the room, her body was shutting down. This is a truly horrible sound you hear at no other time and its meaning is unmistakable. You know what's coming; death is eminent. Along with the medical team, her husband and the rest of her family were in the room. All were aware of what was happening and were thrashing in their powerlessness as they witnessed her final moments. I could feel the struggle she was going through, trying to breath, as though a huge weight was on her chest, crushing her. She was unconscious, but I spoke to her mind to mind.

'Alright then, now's the time. Talk to me.' I opened my perceptions as wide as I could to hear her. There was no need.

Immediately I was flooded with a rush of rage from her such as I have never felt before or since, and the primal, final fear, the fear of ending. The one we all know and fight, bury, and deny every waking moment of our lives. She had no words but she didn't need any, I got it all at once; it was a scream about the unfairness of dying at twenty-one and her dread at facing what she thought was the end. I was wrung to tears in grief and pity at her terror but I forced them away to stay with the business at hand.

'You're right, it's unfair, you have a right to be angry. But you are not dying, and you are not twenty-one. Keep talking, I'm here,' I said, encouraging her, trying to get her to stay with me. I had no idea what I was going to do, but this didn't seem to be the time to think about it, clearly it was time for improvising.

Instantly we flipped to another place, now we were deep in the coalmines of Kentucky. I had no signpost to tell me where we were, I just knew it. It was in the 1930's and I was now with a man in his thirties, a coalminer, and we were in the middle of a cave-in. I looked at the man and I could see the dying girl, their images overlaid on each other, they were the same person. He was very thin and haggard like the girl, but in workman's clothes, wearing a primitive miner's lantern hat and covered with coal dust. We were in a vertical shaft, standing on a narrow ledge. A little residual light was all that could be seen in the confines of the shaft, but it wasn't from the sun. It was red, and powered by a tremendous concussion that blew us both off the ledge. The shaft fell into complete chaos. The walls and the ledge on which we were hanging with our toes and fingernails crumbled around us. The scorching, poisonous gas swept us off the wall and down into the black, seemingly bottomless shaft. We fell into a place of crushing desolation. No light, no life, no beingness; nothing. The coalminer and the girl were being pulled down into the pit. They screamed as they were engulfed in the chaos. I could feel the overwhelming heat and pressure of the explosion. I literally grabbed them by the collar as they swept by me.

'Wait, you are going the wrong way,' I felt swept up into the hurricane, yet I was its eye, calm with chaos around me.

'Lost! I'm lost,' they screamed. 'I don't know where to go! Don't leave me! Come with me,' they howled in unison. The pit hung below us for a moment like a hollow maw, indifferent. Then the first stroke of real fear hit me. 'I can't,' I thought. 'I'll die.' Suddenly I was on a tightrope; one misstep and I would also be lost. I wasn't sure I knew where to go anyway.

'How do you know? You've never tried,' something whispered clearly in my head.

The girl and the coalminer clearly needed my help, and I had never gotten myself into a place like this without getting through it successfully, maybe just by dumb luck, but then maybe not. Still, what if I was wrong? What if I couldn't do it? Was it worth the risk of not being able to get back myself? I finally decided that, if it would help them at all, then it was worth it. Besides, my curiosity always gets the better of me, I always want to know what's behind door number three. All of this was at hyperspeed, it passed though my mind in a millisecond.

'Alright,' I said. Holding my own fear by the throat for a moment, and still holding on to the coalminer and the girl by the back of the collar, I centered my mind on the Light that I could not see, but I knew was there. In the world of thought and energy, the moment you think it, there you are, immediately we were back in the hospital room at the foot of the bed.

The girl's burnt-out body was lying there, its tenant gone. Pure calm had descended, it was done. Sarah was speechless, staring down at her dead body. In a golden ring behind the bed was a group of spirits waiting for her, a legion of the most amazing, loving energy. I could feel their silent welcome as they came to take their daughter home. Their light was extraordinary, pure white and gold. I turned to the spirit that had been known as Sarah in this life and I could see them both, the coalminer and the young woman made of pure white light, as she/he truly was. Even on the level of pure spirit, Sarah was still mute from shock, it was clear that she couldn't believe that such a place existed. In the front row of spirits a matronly woman wearing spectacles and an old-fashioned housedress stepped forward, it felt like her grandmother.

'This is where you were supposed to go. Look at your old body, it was on fire, isn't this much better?' I said to her. We looked at the body in the bed; remnants of fallible clay, it didn't even seem related to this luminous being. All that fighting no longer mattered. Her grandmother extended her hand and I placed her granddaughter's hand in hers.

'*Thank you,*' her grandmother said. Sarah looked at me and said nothing but melted into the ring of gold as she went with them.

'You're welcome. I think.' Suddenly all that had occurred came crashing down on me. I could not believe all I witnessed, it was my turn to be stunned speechless. Without warning I came back to my own awareness and my own body on my couch in my living room. It took a while for my heart to slow down, I thought the blood was going to come out of my ears. I made a note of the time, 2:15 PM. I thought, well, that was pretty darned interesting, tomorrow may show what this all means.

The next day at work I asked where Sarah's sister-in-law, Lauren was, and was told that Sarah had passed away the night before. '*Yea, I know,*' I thought. When Lauren came back from her bereavement leave a week later, I asked what time Sarah had transitioned. The time of death was 2:15 PM on the day I had the vision.

In the following weeks, Lauren and her family did not fare well. Their god was technology, it had not saved them. I had said nothing to her about what I had experienced. I hardly believed it myself. It was becoming clear, though, that something needed to be done. Her brother had to be institutionalized, he had stopped eating and talking to anyone. Lauren admitted to taking Valium just to get through the day. The rest of her family was in the same shape, they were nuking themselves. They just did not have the means to deal with what had happened.

I felt that they were all going to end up in a mental hospital if I didn't say something. I thought about it carefully, they could possibly think I was trying to torture them, but anything had to be better than this. I was very nervous when I finally pulled Lauren aside and told her the story. I prefaced it by saying that she could take it for whatever it was worth to her, and if she wanted to think that I was crazy, that was fine, I would understand. She was silent as she listened, red crept up her face and her eyes watered as I spoke. I found myself having to gulp for air a couple of times while I told her what I had seen. She said nothing for a moment.

'Well…I am not sure I believe you, but I will take this home and tell my family, particularly my brother,' she said slowly. We spoke no more of it. We couldn't, it was too bizarre. I avoided her for a while in the halls, but in a week or so she came to speak to me.

'My brother is better. He's out of the hospital.' I looked at her without speaking; I didn't have the courage to ask for more.

'I told him what you told me. It…helped. I quit taking Valium…my family is…they don't believe it either…but it helped. Thank you.'

'Lauren, it was as much a shock to me as it was to you…' I was still unsure of myself, feeling a need to justify something this weird and not give the impression I was just trying to mock her.

'I'm not sure I believe you, even now…' she said.

'Does it matter? None of us really know the answer, you know…'

She looked at me thoughtfully. 'No…we don't. But thanks.' Here the conversation ended, there was no more to say. Lauren quit her job and moved on soon thereafter.

Who or what had helped Sarah by calling me? A twenty-one year old atheist dying of cancer and a half-trained medical intuitive, neither of us had done anything to warrant such love and support; in the grand scheme of things, we didn't even matter. But I never looked at death the same way again. If this was a gift freely given to us, each just a tiny grain of sand on a beach, who would be left behind?

The Doctors

'Excuse me? You want me to what…?'

The young man sitting in front of me wearing a white coat in the hospital cafeteria had initially struck me as just a young medical resident interested in what I do as a hands-on healer and medical intuitive. Through a lot of hard work, drive and luck, I had received funding to conduct a clinical trial on Reiki at the University of Michigan. The doctor I had been working for saw some merit to test using Reiki to treat diabetic neuropathy, a painful and destructive condition of the feet in Type II diabetes. This was one of the first studies funded by the National Institute of Health in hands-on healing, and my position at the University of Michigan gave me some unique opportunities to interact with the medical staff, which included the residents and fellows. When we met I had immediately categorized the young man as a fairly conventional doctor with some scientific curiosity, nothing more. But what followed certainly goes to show you, it's dangerous to make judgments before getting all of the information.

He looked nothing out of the ordinary, a pleasant young man, studious, bespectacled, about thirty-two years old. He told me that he was a senior resident up in the intensive care unit, and he had just made a very unusual request. It wasn't odd that I was being asked, it just that he, a physician working in one of the oldest, most prestigious teaching hospitals in the world, was doing the asking.

As we sat drinking coffee, he told me that he and a friend were both senior residents in oncology. What this means is that they direct how the second, third and fourth year residents—newly graduated doctors—treat patients, as well as see patients themselves. They, in turn, are supervised and mentored by the attending physicians in their specialty. But at the level this young man functioned on a daily basis, they are practically autonomous. Their hours are long and grueling, and particularly in a hospital of the University of Michigan's size and national ranking, they are exposed to a kind and volume of patient interactions that residents in other hospitals just will not see. It is a tertiary care facility, which means that other hospitals from all over the country, if not the world, send their sickest patients with the rarest diseases there because it has the knowledge and the technology of the highest caliber available to help them. It also nearly guarantees that the quality of these young professionals is beyond comparison to their peers anywhere. They are the best of the best, all of them were at the top of their respective graduating medical school classes in both clinical work and research, and most of them could be classified as brilliant. Many of them have already published in medical journals, some even as undergraduates. That being said, but for a few exceptions, their thinking in terms of healing does not stray far off the main path. So I had expected a general and conservative inquiry at best, and a barely contained argument at worst.

What I got was neither. He explained that he and his fellow resident, a friend of his, frequently supervised what is called a resuscitation code up on the ICU. You have seen this many times on TV; it is the procedure performed on patients when their heart or breathing stops. It is very invasive and violent, first an IV line is rapidly installed, usually in the patient's arm, but anywhere one will go in if there is no other way. The patient is then intubated; a breathing tube about a foot long is inserted into the patient's throat directly down into their lungs with a metal speculum and connected to a mechanical ventilator. The patient is wired to an EKG machine to monitor heart rhythm, of course, if the patient's heart isn't beating, then every alarm on the machine is going off, adding to the noise and chaos. Someone is physically on top of the patient pounding on the heart through the chest wall to passively force the muscle to open and close, thereby keeping a continuous flow of blood going to the brain. Drugs are injected to shock the heart into beating again, to balance the acid-base mixture in the blood, to stop hemorrhaging, to dissolve clots, and for a thousand other reasons. The attending physician is shouting drug concentrations and amounts and the nurses are shouting back in acknowledgment. The defibrillator is used throughout this procedure to initiate an electrical shock to the patient's heart. The paddles are applied, there are shouts of 'Clear!' and everyone stands back for a second while the patient's body nearly arcs off the bed from the electrical current coursing through them.

This can be performed a number of times, but generally after four or five attempts, the heart muscle can no longer conduct current, so it's pretty useless after that. In a last-ditch effort, sometimes the patient's chest is opened with a scalpel, the ribs cracked with bonecutters and spread apart and the heart massaged by hand. The few who are actually resuscitated by this procedure usually don't usually survive for much longer. It's not that these measures don't work, it's just that by the time the patient is so far gone, even when the measures do manage to bring them back, their other organ systems weren't working that well anyway. How long all this lasts is really up to the attending physician. I have seen codes run for as long as 45 minutes, but at that point the patient has been so badly beaten up by the process itself that there isn't much left to work on. So even when successfully resuscitated, the patient has to endure a fairly tortuous process. This is how hard we fight death.

These two young residents ran these "codes" up on the intensive care units, as they are called. This young man dryly said to me, 'It's not good when an oncology patient codes.' I knew what he meant, the patient is usually near death. At that point their hospital stay has been reduced to a waiting game. He told me that they had noticed, particularly when the death occurred after a long illness, or when the patient had resisted the process a great deal, was that they were actually seeing the disembodied energy exit the patient's body during these codes. Often they saw them wandering around the unit, frequently for days, sometimes for much longer, and they wanted to know if I could teach them what to do about it?

I was shocked to speechlessness. I was amazed at the courage of their fearless observations and even more courageous inquiries, particularly in an arena where not only is the very existence of such processes not recognized, but also in many cases, the intellectual environment is openly hostile toward them.

I sat and listened as this quiet, studious-looking young man told me of stories in which he and his colleague had watched and even felt the pain and confusion radiating from these spirits who had left their bodies and didn't know where to go.

Much to his surprise and relief, I had a solution, and I wasn't the first one to think of it, either. All of the religions of the world are familiar with this issue and have ritualized protocols already in place for just such occurrences. Even the Western Christian traditions have such rituals, although the general population knows very little about them. Unless the hospital has a chaplain or priest on duty who understands the concept, the physical building can get rather congested, due to the accumulation of lost spirits. Have you ever gone into a hospital and felt uncomfortable or even claustrophobic? You've probably written it off as your own discomfort or even that you were around suffering people, but it may be those who have been thrown out of their bodies suddenly from a rough leave-taking are lost, and cannot find the exit. It's just a little busy in there. The older hospitals can feel like an airport that has had all of the planes grounded for the last fifty years.

This young doctor explained that although he also felt and saw these energies wandering around, his colleague was the one really plagued by them. He was not frightened of these lost spirits; he just wanted to know what to do about them. The doctors were very busy, but agreed to meet in a few weeks time, out in the campus' arboretum and talk the matter over.

We met quite some time later. March in Michigan, is a beautiful spot in springtime. New azaleas, rhododendrons and roses, all carefully tended sent an array of wonderful scents into the air, surrounded us as we settled down on the grass. It was fitting in that talking about death and dying, we were surrounded by a new cycle of life, and also within view of the children's hospice.

The other resident was more intense than the first young man, but just as intelligent and observant. Taller and more imposing, with a shock of red hair, his two young boys were with him, playing at our feet. The elder boy, about four, gave evidence of his father's abilities being hereditary, he watched me with a peculiar look, one older than his years.

The young man went on to explain what was happening to him. It was clear that his ability to see, hear, and feel energies around him was accelerating, becoming stronger everyday. What is particularly fascinating is that he could recall exactly when it started. At one point in his medical training he had become very ill. Diagnosed with meningitis, he had experienced a very high fever that had been sustained for days. He didn't remember much of it, but when he returned to work, he started to see things. Flickering and popping energies, some in various colors, but mostly white, much like the way I see energy now. Once, when he was working on a patient during a code, he felt a tremendous influx of energy. From that point on, his hands frequently ended up pulsing and getting very hot when working on patients. This is very common of hands-on healers; Reiki, Therapeutic Touch, Polarity, Healing Touch, all of us describe the same phenomenon. I have it happen to me often, as I mentioned, it began during my years as a member of an ambulance team.

What you do about all this is actually rather simple. We are spiritual beings with the power and authority to direct a transitioning spirit where they need to go. This has been bourn up by centuries of written records about rituals with the dying. You can ask for angelic or spiritual help, but it's mostly a bit like what happened with Sarah, you just visualize the residual spiritual energy going to the right place. Sometimes all it takes is a gentle reminder that their physical body is dead and the inhabitant needs to move on to the next level. If you can't do that, then a simple prayer for their safe passage is all that's needed and the belief that they will be cared for.

It was obvious that these young men were very powerful, but there were several other things that seemed clear. I was struck to the heart by the fact that they both knew exactly what their role was; to help people find healing in whatever way worked best for them, even if that meant transition. Not by euthanasia, I don't believe that is in our hands. I mean by being there and being a steady energy that can reassure a frightened patient that all will be well, no matter what the outcome. It is the emotional connection that matters.

But what also occurred to me like a thunderbolt is that these two young men, in this milieu, needed my experience. This was part of the reason I was here, now, in this place at this University. This meeting may have been planned before all of us were born, as set in stone as the coming of spring. My illness, path to healing and years of research had almost been secondary to this meeting, all had led up to this point. The next generation of healers was on their way, perhaps these young men could lead their dying patients to a greater understanding about the dying process. Working in this field at the University had been arduous, but I could see now had a purpose, my work here was almost done.

Anya

All my life I have been afraid of trains. Not passenger trains, or at least not after I get on them, if I can run from the platform up the steps, then I'm fine. I'm afraid of black freight trains. My mother used to love to ride the train when I was little, and I would scream and fight her like a drowning cat while we were boarding. This never changed, I was as afraid of them at eight as I was at three, although I was better able to control myself by then. She had asked me in exasperation what I was afraid of, and of course, as a three-year old has no way of explaining how this feels, so I couldn't say, but it felt like Ending. Once I was on board it would be over, but only after convincing everyone within earshot that I was being tortured. She was completely frustrated by my behavior but nothing she did could get me to stop.

To this day I don't like trains or subway platforms, although I can manage my anxiety if I stand well back from the door until it has stopped. But my real phobia is black freight trains, and since this is not something you run into everyday, like heights or snakes, I don't think about it much.

But where did this come from? I was one of those kids who would figuratively go over Niagara Falls in a barrel, run to the edge of a cliff and look down to catch the view and play chicken on the freeway at 95 mph when I was in my twenties. Obviously this got me into no end of trouble, but for much of it, I lived the life of the charmed. I had even asked my mother at one point if a train had scared her somehow when she was pregnant with me; she said no. But I finally got my answer, or at least some very interesting clues about it in my thirties when I was touring an industrial museum that featured a collection of full-sized trains.

An observation seems pertinent here; I have always felt very "tall" in this life. As to height, I am 5'7", slightly taller than the average American woman which I believe is 5'2", but certainly not up in the oxygen seats. Many women and almost all men are taller than me. I have just always felt very high up off the ground. I don't mind it, as a matter of fact I rather like it, but this impression has been with me all of my life.

Not having been around a train for years, I had completely forgotten about this particular phobia until I went to this train museum with a friend. Wandering aimlessly, we weren't paying attention to where we were walking, when suddenly I realized we were in the midst of a multitude of trains, hundreds of cars linked together, blocking me in. Terror hit me again in full force, I felt like I was three years old again. It didn't help that these trains were black, and most of them those old-fashioned, wooden-slatted freight cars.

I was white as a sheet and I felt myself alternately sweating hot and cold. I could walk between the rows if one were shorter than the other and provided a way out, but when confronted with two very long rows, I absolutely could not do it. I could tolerate being between the rows for only about a second. My friend, who knows me to be pretty fearless, thought I had lost my mind.

When you've been an active addict, there's very little that scares you anymore. You've been to the bottom, so you learn fear is just another emotion, and it will not kill you. There has also been that part of me that is the scientist/observer, and standing one side of this fear and looking in, I was fascinated by it and wanted to know what was causing it. It felt like death, black, all consuming and absolutely endless. The other thing I have learned about fear is that, like all things, this too shall pass. So I decided to confront this lifelong mystery and see what would happen.

While I couldn't quite bring myself to climb into a freight car, that was a wall I could not pass, I could climb into one of the locomotives. This particular one had the back wall cut out and a window installed so that you could look into the freight car behind it as an example of a mass transport vehicle of the times, this one fitted out to haul livestock. There was straw on the floor, light and dust-moted air trickled in through the slats. The loading doors were shut.

The moment I turned around and looked through the window into the freight car and a vision hit me so strongly I knew I had been there. I was in the middle of a flashback; a hundred sensations came to me in a rush.

Cold…freezing, bitter cold. This was so cold my teeth were chattering, it went through and instantly drew every ounce of warmth from me. They were chattering so badly that I thought I was going to break a tooth. Small, short, I felt short, and tiny, perhaps 4'10" and about 85 lbs, no bigger than a child. Was I a child? I looked down at my clothes, no. I was an adult woman, just very small. But I could also see myself from the outside as well, I was very fair with blond hair and blue eyes. If you had ever met me you would know how impossible this is. As I mentioned, I am of medium/tall height, an olive-skinned brunette with brown eyes. I may have been less than 5 foot tall at some point but I have never been a fair-skinned blond with blue eyes.

I was overwhelmed by claustrophobia. I was completely pinned. I couldn't move. I was packed in with other people so tightly that no one could change position. Despite the fact that it was so cold, I felt suffocated, there was no air, or very little. I could barely see over other people's heads around me, but I could see that I was in the middle of a black freight car.

Anya was a name I recognized and felt like it was mine. Yes, Anya, the Polish nickname for Anna. I knew very strongly that we were in Poland, that I was Polish and it was winter. When, what year felt hazier. Somewhere in the late 1930's, perhaps the early forties, other people's clothing looked like from about that time period, as did mine. I was wearing a brown dress with a wide white collar with big brown buttons and brown sling back shoes, such as were popular in that time period. My knees ached and I longed to lie down, to this day I have arthritic knees, although I have never been an athlete. Many, many people were crammed in the car. What I could see of the passing countryside was deep forest, snow-covered, beautiful in its silence and austerity. Very deep snow, isolation, both inside and out.

What was strongest was the feeling of just waiting for the last breath to be drawn. If I had any will at all, it was to die on this trip, wherever we were going. I knew I had children, and they were gone. They had been taken away from me and sent on another train to somewhere else, but I knew they were already dead. I knew I was going to die and it couldn't happen soon enough. Complete despair, and where there is despair, there is no light, only the desire for extinction, and the merciful loss of memory. The only other thing was the clacking of the wheels on the tracks and the swaying motion of the train. No one spoke, with the exception of the occasional word when someone stepped on someone else.

That was all. I don't remember getting off the train. I remember very vaguely seeing an empty car and piles of bodies, very many, stacked in a brick-laid freight yard. I could see a multitude of feet sticking out. Mine were among them. I had lost a shoe.

Later I saw a film clip of the train yard at Auschwitz, the most notorious of the World War II Nazi prison camps and that sense of inward chill again hit me, like when a memory is slow in coming, not like a lightning bolt, just that slow, creeping recognition that you've been there.

My own belief is that it is from a memory of my own from another life. I have other memories that are as clear as the ones from the life I'm living now and yet I know they are not from this time period. I love Russian symphonic music, I'm fascinated by the Russian Revolution and I can tell you details about the interior of the Winter Palace in what is now once again St. Petersburg, although I've never been there in this life. I haven't read "War and Peace," either. There have been people in this life who I have met and known from first sight that this is just another chapter in a continuing story, and they have felt the same way. Places where I have stood and known that I have stood there before. Not just "déjà vu," momentary glimpses or feelings of having been there before, but full blown distinct memories of places and persons. You look in their eyes, you don't recognize their face, but their soul and yours are saying in unison, 'Hello, where ya been?'

All of this is debatable, of course. There is no proof within this frame of reference, so there's no point in getting into that particular argument. But most of the spiritual paths of the world believe in the "recycling" of souls with the exception of the Christian tradition, although in the writings of St Jerome, he talks about the "transmigration of souls" in which souls are reborn from life to life. There have literally been thousands of stories recorded cross-culturally over centuries of these kinds of memories.

As a child, I was skeptical of the "one soul per person" theory; if my rate of learning how to be a good person remained the same, then the chances of my attaining "heaven" were, from my point of view, pretty small. How could I possibly learn all of this in one lifetime?

Good grief, my parents weren't even close to perfect, and I knew I wasn't! How was I going to do it? So when I encountered the possibility of reincarnation, it seemed reasonable to me. This issue has never been a matter of faith, it was the result of being pragmatic. When the evidence doesn't fit, examine other explanations. Like Sherlock Holmes, no matter how preposterous that theory might be, until more evidence becomes available, that is your working theory. Any other way just seems like a waste of energy, and despite our belief that the Christian belief is the predominant belief system in the world, in reality, the majority of the rest of humanity believe in the recycling of souls. Who's to say they're wrong?

If reincarnation is not true, then it is the one exception to the patterns of everything else that exists. Energy, matter, it's never lost, it just transforms, everything is recycled, Einstein's equation. Certainly other conclusions can be made based on these experiences, and I agree that some other explanation may be as valid. But crazy is as crazy does, and until I observe evidence to the contrary, I believe that there are other lives and other times that I have lived. Many people have been born with birthmarks recognized by people in their former families and distinct memories of other times and other lives, even as early as 2 years old. As to whether you have lived other lives before the one you are living now, you must make up your mind for yourself.

As to Anya's fate in the camps and the millions like her, even now, you'd think we would have gotten that part right by now. She still sees through my eyes now and then, I can feel her there, and she remembers. She cannot forget.

Here to There

This story is about dying, to be sure, but perhaps from a longer perspective. We must face the possibility as a species as well as individually. In between birth, death and immortality, there is the washing and the ironing, isn't there?

Three weeks after September 11th, 2001, I was about to begin a Reiki session on a client who is a first generation Japanese-American, Carol Yamasaki. All of us were still pretty much shell-shocked, Carol and I had talked about this before we began the session. The burning images of the collapsing towers kept looping in our collective mind, I could feel it. From my experience nothing happens in a vacuum, cause and effect is unavoidable, but there are times when you are definitely reminded you were not named supervisor of the Universe any time recently. That was the only answer I had for her, there weren't any guarantees that we would ever find out why this had happened.

A healing session begins by the practitioner taking a few minutes to relax and focus and I was having a hard time doing this. I was going to have to find a way to let these images go, at least temporarily. As I asked to connect to that energy that allows me to do my work, I also asked for some way of putting in perspective what we had all just seen and heard, and seemingly lost.

Immediately I heard a voice say very compassionately but detached, resonant, clear,

'This doesn't matter, you know.' Aside from feeling shock at being spoken to directly, my response was immediate.

'What do you mean, this doesn't matter, thousands of people died in that attack, are you crazy? Of course it matters!' I heard the voice again.

'Not to them, it doesn't. Most of them didn't even realize what happened. It only hurt for a second, they're all fine now.'

'Well, it matters to their relatives then!' I had been haunted by the thought of how many people had no resolution, no visit from the police, no body, no nothing. Their loved ones just never came home.

'More understand than you think.'

Ascending into another level, I again saw the images of the falling towers, but this time they were pure white rimmed in gold, they gleamed in the sun as they fell. The buildings were a chrysalis, a sacred place, a place of accelerated evolutionary motion. There were millions upon millions of souls watching as the buildings crumbled. The building occupants changed form and just simply stepped out and joined their companions in spirit. It was a joyous meeting, a celebration, multi-colored balloons and confetti flying into the starlit expanse and crowds cheering in welcome, they had come home a hard and fast road. The images were shifting so rapidly, I had no time to be amazed.

The scene flipped, I was now myself out in the enormity of space. The Sun and his mighty train of followers, the planets were all laid out before me on the black velvet of limitless space marked with the twinkling of the living stars. It brought tears to my eyes, it was so beautiful, I realized with a rush of joy, this is our home.

But something marred the view, I became aware of a horrible stench, it was choking me. I was reminded sharply of a smell that I used to chance upon when I was working as an EMT. When there is a very bad car accident, particularly if one or more of the cars have burned, there is an odor at the scene that is very distinctive. The smell is of burning oil, radiator coolant, rubber, plastic, blood, and one more thing, if there were occupants trapped in the burning vehicles, the smell of burning meat. It is a very penetrating odor, it stays with your clothes your hair, your mouth, you never forget as long as you live. It didn't make any sense at first, but I could smell that now, out in the boundless expanse of space.

The Earth was outside of my field of vision, but as I slowly came around the sun and my perspective widened, a brown marble, streaked with black and pockmarked slag came into view. It was still slowly spinning, but the day and the night now fell on it without meaning. The bitterness of the burnt-out fire was in my mouth and I fought the realization that this was the source of the stench. I nearly vomited from despair when the realization hit me that this was the Earth. My heart and mind were slapped into complete silence. I heard the voice again.

'This is what you can do to yourselves in 17 minutes. This is not a given, this is only one road. These people gave up their lives so that you could understand that you have another choice. You can do this, or you can choose to understand that you are all in this together. It is up to you.'

The scene flipped back to the two towers in white and gold and the souls who had just left it, whom I knew now, had done what they did knowingly on some level to change that line of possibilities. But this time, a rather short Japanese man, was standing next to the towers. He gesticulated to the buildings and then to me rather impatiently, and then he spoke.

'This is what these were designed for, this was their purpose, to change our path,' he said.

Now I was confused, who was this man? He looked sort of like my client, Carol. There the vision ended, and I came back to the room where she was lying on the table waiting for me. I told her what I had seen, described the little Japanese gentleman and asked her if she knew who he was. She bolted upright on the table, her eyes wide and her face pale.

'That was my father, Minori Yamasaki. He designed the World Trade Center Towers.'

We were both stunned. All I know is that human nature being what it is, we rarely learn the lesson easily or remember it for long. It may get worse before it gets better, but perhaps a longer view may be in order. We have a Winter so Spring can come.

The Bird

Since this is a book about healing, a discussion of dying invariably becomes a discussion about living. Even in the face of death, I have been witness to healings that defy all conventional explanations. So even when all seems lost, that is merely our perception, and while our beliefs might be the hardest things in the world to change, they really are very easy, given the right circumstances. Sometimes all you need is an open mind.

When I was living in Michigan, I had a lovely Cape Cod bungalow near the University. It was really in the city, but it was on a large piece of land with a small woods behind it, so it gave the illusion of being out in the country. One day several years ago I was sitting in my sunroom looking out onto the woods on a beautiful day in June, it was the last day of spring before the fireburst of summer. There is nothing like it if you have never experienced summer in the Midwest, muted and more subtle in its way, but it has an energy that is uniquely its own. Every color has been washed and brushed and is strutting its stuff, the skies change from moment to moment.

Those who lived in my backyard were always nesting, foraging, flying or singing, nothing was ever still. The squirrels were the size of cats and they drove the neighborhood dogs crazy. The birds were legion, jays and robins, brilliant red cardinals, woodpeckers of every kind, crows, hawks hunting for mice, even the occasional owl if you were lucky. Watching the flow of traffic one day, I spotted two tiny woodpeckers, one chasing the other, two little fighter jets blazing toward the sunroom window off the back porch. They were not paying attention, so when they both hit the window, it rang like a gong. For a second I thought it was going to break, but it didn't.

Both of them hit the wooden deck like rocks. I bolted outside, I thought they must be dead, but no, one had already struggled into lopsided flight, no doubt seeing stars. The second one had also tried to launch an escape, but as his luck would have it, which was decidedly not good today, he hit the porch railing and again hit the deck. I flinched, you could hear the whack he made against the railing, this time the blood flew.

I ran over and picked him up, a rush of bird size terror blew off him, I knew he thought he was dying. He was probably right, he was bleeding from his mouth, just a few drops, but probably the equivalent to one of us losing several pints. But that was not the most alarming injury he had incurred, his neck and head quite simply stuck out at a 45° angle.

As an energy healer, you are working with what is really true, so very little is impossible. But you have to let go of how it will accomplish what you ask of it. I didn't know what I wanted to ask, so I covered the bird with my hands and ran down to the grass below and sat down to think. My hands were shaking, at that time I did not feel adept at healing work, I was just a student. I could feel his heart thundering; it felt like this little bit of feathers in my hands was going to explode.

Time was of the essence, I could see him through the web of my fingers; he was dying, something had to be done now. I didn't know what I could do for him, but I knew intuitively that I had to ramp up the energy quickly, so to calm down and force myself to focus, I began to sing "Amazing Grace." It qualified at that moment as the only song to which I could remember the words. I would have sung "Jingle Bells" if I could have remembered the words, but at that moment I was so rattled, I couldn't.

There is nothing special about my voice, a rusty alto, it is permanently lowered by cigarettes even though I no longer smoke, and when I get nervous I can't hold the key. But by focusing on the music, something different started happening this time, the immediate area around us began to change with a shimmering pulse that you really couldn't see, but you could feel. It was as if this reality is only a veneer, a cover for deeper truth that we were breaking through together, this little bird and me.

I kept singing, the pulse increased, a pleat in time occurred, it began to run backwards, that's the only way I can describe it. I could feel the energy pulsing off my hands being amplified by the vibration of my voice, and as powerfully as a locomotive and gentle as a whisper, I watched frozen in awe as it gently twisted the bird's neck and head back to its normal position. There were no cheers of hallelujah, no angelic beings appeared; it simply went back into place.

The shimmering dissipated, I slowly opened my hands and he sat there, perfect, like a little Buddha, barred wings, red feathered cap and black kerchief around his throat, ruffling and smoothing his feathers and cocking his head as he listened to me sing. There was no mark on him, no blood. I kept singing and we sat together for 20 minutes, no one in the world but us. I stopped, and then as suddenly as snapping out of a hypnotic trance, he came to awareness of me, and shooting a look of surprise and some indignation, flew off in a flash.

I knew that music could increase the energy in an area and amplify the intent of the musician, but I had never seen anything like this. The bird was mortally injured; yet he flew away perfect. It was as if it had never been.

I know the light we never think we see, it shines inside, yet it is so elusive. It is a secret, yet it's right in front of us, in all we see. What I do know is that the sound of it is music. It is ours for the asking, in everything we do, even down to saving the life of the tiniest bird. But when will we finally see and hear, and when will we know?

Choices

I'm fairly sure this story also may qualify as my final doctoral defense, but since I'm always trying to stay curious, I've had no indication I'm done yet. There were so many things that happened that were the culmination of what I had learned so far, that's how I think of this one. All I know is that it was a far cry from that lonely, confused girl of so many years ago, but it certainly wasn't my doing. Exactly why this happened when it did, for both Alan and myself is something I'm still trying to figure out.

No one knows why the Sphinx was built. The experts can't even decide when it was built, research sets the time as early as 10,000 years ago and the latest estimate at 3000 years ago. I felt that there were rooms under the Sphinx, somehow knowing I had been there. When or how, I can't tell you. But they are there, they were used in ritual practice. Ritual is used to invoke energy for a number of purposes; praying is ritual. We have been given the ability to invoke this energy in many ways, through music, dance, and language, to access the unseen. We may not recognize it as such, but we still do this. The essence of non-dual time and space is not accessed by the intellect alone, it must be accessed through the heart.

One day several years ago, I was working with energy on one of my oldest clients with Reiki as I usually do. I worked on him regularly for chronic pain in his feet for many years. Alan, a short, slightly heavy retired electrician was saddled with diabetes and a heart condition. He was no major intellect, but that didn't matter. He was a compassionate, thinking man, full of common sense and had led a good life. He had been Regina's husband, the woman whose story I told earlier.

Alan had experienced a major heart attack about eleven years previously, which had left a portion of his left ventricle—the business end of the pump—about the size of a quarter, dead and his cardiac output consequently diminished.

This had been verified by an echocardiogram after his surgery to correct the coronary circulation, I had seen the pictures. An echocardiogram is exactly what it sounds like, it's a sonar map of the interior of the heart. Sometimes these types of surgery have to be redone, or least supported with angioplasty, sort of a plumbing job on the heart vessels. Unfortunately as a diabetic and because of his advanced age, Alan was not a good risk for even an awake procedure like angioplasty. So this Reiki session was to focus on his heart, to see if we could allay the accumulation of arterial plaque that was slowly strangling it, and to strengthen the deadened area. A "quarter-sized" area is a considerable amount of tissue loss, much more than that and the patient's heart cannot sustain adequate pump efficiency to stay alive.

In energy work, sometimes you pick the moment, but sometimes the moment picks you. When I focused on centering and put my hands on him, the energy hit me like a tidal wave. Usually the build-up is slower and feels hot or cold, pulsing or more wavelike. It seems to vary according to the patient's need, you as the practitioner are only the conduit, like with the little bird, the energy knows what to do. This time it was like instantly being in a sauna and was pulsing so hard that my own heart rate immediately kicked up to over 120 beats per minute. Within minutes, sweat was dripping off my hair and down my back.

Suddenly the scene before me shifted rapidly; I found myself in the desert at the edge of the Nile in Egypt, but with my back to the river, facing the gigantic lion-human form of the Sphinx. The Great Pyramids hung in the background, their huge sloping shoulders bearing their own secrets, oblivious to the relentless beat of the sunlight. I knew intuitively that the Sphinx in front of me held the greatest, immutable secret of all. I knew that the basis of strength for them all was the same, but this monument was the foundation. Historians and other learned people have debated its purpose, and since there is no written record of it, it is often ascribed as a tribute to Ramses the Great. Ironically, this was the pharaoh who was convinced by a greater magic than his to free the Jews from slavery.

I was struck not only by its immensity and age as I stared at its looming form, but also by some sort of expectancy, its lips pursed shut. I felt like it wanted to tell me what its secret was, or rather, that its secret was obvious and it was very funny that no one had gotten it.

Our own research and records are entangled with an unconscious arrogance and bias that only this culture can elicit and the dead cannot contradict. We automatically think that our culture is the culmination, the apex of civilization and that earlier cultures were ignorant and superstitious compared to us. Perhaps in some ways they have not been as advanced technologically as we are, but there may have existed areas of inquiry that we can only guess at.

As I was standing about 100 feet away from the Sphinx's right shoulder and forepaw, I felt nearly crushed by the ferocious heat of the Sahara. The sand, the blinding sunlight and azure sky, all winding down to the green oasis down by the river and the ancient Nile, a silver-blue ribbon, laid out before me.

In a vision, it's as real as your hand in front of your face, this one was no exception, I could feel the sand under my feet, the hot wind as it whipped my hair around my face, the overwhelming brightness of the landscape.

My perspective then suddenly flip-flopped. It was now clear that I was looking from an elevated perspective, but not so very different from the one before. The scenery had shifted slightly, I was now facing the river with my back to the Pyramids, the Sphinx no longer in view. As I turned to the right, I saw a human body lying in the sand not far away. It seemed very tiny, it looked familiar, it was a woman, with long, black hair swirled in the sand, obscuring her face. It was me, and I knew that body was dead. You'd think that seeing your own dead body would be unsettling, but it wasn't. It was as simple as seeing an old pair of discarded jeans that have worn out, and not even that much feeling was attached to it. It meant nothing at all to me; an old story, now done.

As I turned my head back, the first things I saw extended before me were two huge paws…with claws. I startled slightly and in doing so, realized that the paws belonged to me, because they jumped when I did. The analytical part of my head kicked in and just started taking it in like a computer analyzing data. As I turned to look and started flexing my muscles, trying to figure out what had happened, chunks of sandstone started flaking away from my body. With a slow but calm realization, I realized I had become the Sphinx. A tawny lion's body with golden fur and strong, elegant muscles was coming out of the outer sand casing, I could feel the energy this body was drawing up from the earth like a power cord; dense, smooth, enough to move mountains.. I got the sense of being a part of the earth, possessing raw, undirected, ancient power. The head and face, surrounded by the Egyptian cowl in black and gold and lapis was that of a woman, me. Picture the mask of Tutankhamen, although it was most definitely my head and face, but alive with my mind behind it as well, alive and sensing, thinking and integrating. The only difference was that there were three black stripes running diagonally across my face from nose to jawline on both sides. I came to find out later that the original Sphinx also had these markings but the paint had been worn away by time.

Now some more background is necessary here, what was happening is known as "shapeshifting." This is an old tradition, or ability, and exists in most esoteric paths and nature religions in one form or another. One takes on the form of an animal usually, or part of one, or several blended together. It is a natural talent, everyone can do it, but many people can only do it in the dream state, some only by accident, and a few by willing it in an awake state, usually with training. Some do it for pleasure, others for a purpose. But there is one caveat that one must observe, one must be very disciplined and only use it when needed, because the longer you stay in animal form, the more like that animal you become. It can be very seductive. Being an animal gives you different abilities, you generally pick the animal that gives you the qualities you wish to possess for the task at hand, or rather, it picks you. This can be a lot of fun, but you also take on the mental perspective of that animal, so the motivation to go back to your human form fades, to the point of forgetting that you were ever human at all. Then you are stuck in that form for the rest of your life and your human body dies. I have heard of this happening but have never seen it, but when you shapeshift yourself, the attraction to stay in your chosen form is very strong.

There was really no danger of that this time, as my mind was still human, but possessing a lion's body was definitely influencing my perspective. A lion is a meat eater. They chase their prey down and kill it. Life and death are pragmatic matters. Predators must kill to survive; there is no remorse involved. It's their nature, that of survival. Neither is it "bad" or "wrong," it just is what it is. It is ruthless in a way, but knowing when a thing's time to die has come takes discernment, as well as knowing when it's time to be born. Even predators themselves return to the earth when their lives are done.

So it was this kind of perspective that allowed me to see what I saw. Kaleidoscopic, at least a dozen perspectives presented themselves to me. I saw all of the patterns of the earth, the living and the dying, the weather changes, cultures arising and falling into dust, the cyclical nature of all of it, everything in balance. Very violent changes are inherent in all of it, yet I could see that it was all a part of the same turning wheel.

This was pure animal power, earth power, able to change and move anything material, but undirected, focused only on the cyclical nature of all life. There was also pure human intellect; I was still part human. I knew that with my consciousness and creativity directing the energy, I could manifest any intention I wished with the power at my command. The blending of all of these qualities is absolutely necessary in the manifestation of intention, something that only we as human beings can do. Here was the secret; we have the power through intention, of harnessing the power of all that is. We understand this to a small degree, but have lost the concept of working within the cycle.

As I stood up, twitching my fur to shake off the last of the sand, I walked down to the river; part animal and part human, in possession of raw power, pure detached intellect and pure compassion. The juncture between art, magic and healing is something we have lost, we don't understand that when a thing is beautiful, very likely it has many purposes as well.

As I watched the river flow north, again I warped into several perspectives at the same time. One was exactly where I was, a woman-lion pacing the Nile, another was in my healing room at home standing over my client, and yet a third was out in space somewhere talking to Alan in spirit. Our brains can really process a great deal more than we give them credit for or allow them to do, and you can keep it all straight with a little practice, but it's definitely difficult to describe.

I was in a conversation with him, both of us were looking at the illusion of his damaged heart. I recognized immediately that he had chosen this energy pattern as a way of opting out of his life at this time if he wished. Since his love for himself—we all must have love for ourselves to be healthy—was diminished, he had unknowingly shut off this energy to his heart.

Interestingly, many people do this. It's part of the reason—that and our diet—we have so much heart disease in this culture. So in the world of pure energy and intention, Alan's healing was merely a matter of changing his intention. One thing I had finally learned, however, is that he must do it, I couldn't do it for him. Being responsible for our own intentions, both productive and nonproductive, is the key.

Either decision he made was fine, to stay or to leave, it was only a change of energy patterns. Beside the picture of his heart as the damaged illusion, I showed him a picture of what his heart really looked like, perfect, and then spoke to him mind to mind.

'This is what you think your heart looks like and this is what it really looks like, it's completely whole. If you remain with the damaged version, then you will leave this plane and go to the next one within a short period.' I could see three more months in one possible timeline.

'If you choose the second one, then you will remain here for a while longer.' That timeline had at least 8 more years in it, perhaps more.

'There are no wrong answers, but it is your choice. What do you want?'

'If I choose to leave, will I still be able to see my children?' He asked.

'Yes, but they will not be able to see you. Because they are still tied to the plane you currently recognize as the only one that exists, they will experience your leaving as a loss.'

'But I miss my wife. I want to see her again.' It would be a struggle for him, I knew. Regina had passed a few years before and he still missed her terribly; his grief had not lessened. I could see standing right beside him, but he wasn't ready for that knowledge, so he couldn't see her. She motioned me to silence about her presence, he had to make this decision by himself.

'I know you miss her. But again, I cannot make this decision for you. What do you want?' I held both pictures in balance for him, waiting for the answer.

He replied slowly and emphatically, 'I choose to stay.'

In the place where the truth is, when the inner intention is changed, the outer view responds immediately. Several things started happening at once, the most notable was the initiation of an energy flow from my heart to his and the presence of a set of musical harmonics. It seemed to be coming through my heart from the energy that is All That Is. When you speak the truth, it is induced it back to its "root vibration."

The picture of his heart as perfect overwhelmed and subsumed the picture of his old, defective organ, I was then suddenly flipped back to my healing room.

I have gotten used to the slight dizziness experienced upon returning my physical body, but sometimes it takes the person you're working on a bit longer to readjust. I felt very…small. Rats, I was going to miss being a lion. Alan also appeared to be coming back from wherever he had been. Both of us were sweating and very, very hot, but he seemed awed and subdued.

'What…was that?' Clearly something had happened to him as well but he didn't seem consciously aware of his decision to stay. I admired his choice. All of us get that choice at one point or another in our lives, and not everyone makes the choice he did. It takes courage to stay here, this is something we all know.

'I'm not sure,' I said, 'But I think we're going to find out. How do you feel?'

'Great, just fine.' He seemed puzzled but willing to go along with whatever was happening. He was used to me by now. When I asked him later if he saw or heard anything, he said no.

He was scheduled to go in and get another echocardiogram performed on his heart, which he did. His results came back perfect, at the bottom of the set of images was written by the physician, "I have no explanation for these results." No doubt.

Alan and I laughed in delight about this for a long time. We knew what had happened, but we also knew no one would believe us. We just felt honored that we had been given the opportunity to look into the heart of these matters. It didn't matter that no one knew.

Alan passed away about eight years after this happened, over time, his heart vessels slowly blocked again. But there is something I have come to know from my experience with Alan: "Reality" is a balance between engaging and letting go, but it is our intention that is the fulcrum. What do you want?

The Mirrored Candle

All laid before me in an instant and all time was now. Suddenly I was everything, from the tiniest grain of sand to within the molecules of the birth of stars. I could see everything, the Earth and its flora and fauna, man and woman as we developed on this planet, our history, the great wars, from spears and arrows to the boom of artillery and the mushroom of mass destruction, even the evolution of life in other systems. I was not only observing these things but I also was those events, and those animals and peoples. Cycle after cycle presented itself, souls coming in and going out of the dance. There was no emotion attached to any of it, except the hum of the Universe, the sound it makes, which is a song that goes on forever, a limitless place where everything, every time, is now.

A pure energy runs through all things. Death and life are an innate part of it, there is no thing outside of this energy. It is beyond love and hate. There is no fear, that is nowhere outside of ourselves, an illusion that we have constructed. Fear is based on the concept that we are limited and we have not, and that has no meaning, because we are made up of the very material that the stars are made of, all falls under the lens of our intention.

I watched planets as they spun off gargantuan suns, bits of molten metal, saw peoples and histories on foreign planets rise and fall, explosions of stars, watched as far away galaxies were born, danced in awe and joy as the pattern of all things revealed itself. It's an endless Moebius strip, looping on itself, no beginning and no ending.

I thought of all the people I knew, those I loved and those I thought had opposed me, and in that instant I was seeing from their perspective. I saw their lives, past and present, like an overlay, faces and lives and timelines diverging and converging. It's a strange thing to witness, all the things we are. But in that moment I developed real empathy, for I saw the fear and the isolation that we all labor under everyday. It is the idea that we walk this life separate and alone, and that we each knock on the final door of death by ourselves. That is the illusion; none of these things are real. The matrix that binds us is one fabric, there is no "other." It's all one thing, no one or thing is outside of this vast array of experiences known as life, it's all there for the asking. Those who had opposed me had done so out of the mistaken idea that I had the power to take something away from them, or they wanted something they thought I had. In All That Is, that idea has no meaning.

I thought of other worlds, and as I've said before, in the world of thought and energy, the moment you think it, there you are. Instantly I was in another physical dimension on a planet very far away. If there were laws of gravity, that's not how I would have explained them. There was no "up" or "down," it was only "here." I became aware that I was in the presence of a creature half my height; the basis of their physical matrix, I think, was silicon rather than carbon, it resembled something vaguely out of Dr. Seuss. I didn't want to be rude, but I was trying hard not to laugh. I thought he was very funny-looking, he was sort of a pastel-green and rather pudgy, but I knew I must have looked just as funny to this little creature.

We spoke wordlessly, or rather because we were of the same matrix and were each other, we knew instantly, pure communication, no ego, no masks, no dust thrown in the eyes, just authentic connection. We almost never get that here, but it's as comfortable as a pair of old shoes. They know everything about you and you know everything about them, and it's all fine, pure acceptance. I saw a soul like mine, the same lessons and the same path, just a different context.

You mustn't get the idea that this was all drama and seriousness, I was as thrilled and happy as a kid on roller blades, zooming around, the Universe is pure music and laughter, you can't help but join in. You don't have to take lessons to learn how to fly, you are born knowing.

Many years ago I had a vision of talking to Jesus. I had been raised Catholic but I had gone through a period when I started down this path of questioning my handed-down beliefs. I was starting over from the beginning at this point. I am truly a skeptic. Years before this vision, though, I had been at a retreat and I had considered the question, 'Who was this Jesus, and why had he come here?' Well, the Universe will always answer your questions, you just have to be open to the answer.

One of my first visions came in a meditation at a retreat. In it, I saw a man in white walking towards me. His energy was tremendous, radiating all around him, but very gentle, all in white-gold. Still, I had a hard time believing he was who I suspected he was. I look back on it now and think that it was screamingly obvious; I just couldn't believe he had come through for *me*.

'Uh…who…who are you???' I asked. I was stuttering, I was so freaked out.

'Who do you think I am?' The man smiled.

'Are you Jesus?'

He smiled again and said nothing, and then to use a terrible cliché, I got blinded by the Light. Emanating from this being was the most intense energy, light and love that I had ever experienced. When you are at that level of energy, physical boundaries become meaningless, and I felt myself merging with him and All That Is. There was no such thing as other, it was all One. I was not ready for such love and connection yet, so I panicked. I felt I was losing who I was in the onslaught.

'Stop, I can't handle it!' He pulled his energy back immediately.

'OK,' he said, still smiling gently.

'Thanks…thanks, I…thank you, I just can't handle that level of energy yet.' I felt ridiculous for refusing.

'OK, you…you are…him…' I couldn't even say his name.

'I am always here…'

'OK…thanks.' I avoided looking at him, I wasn't too sure I was comfortable with the idea of seeing Jesus, either. This vision had really scared me. He slowly faded out before me, but I thought about it for a long time afterwards.

So now we come forward again to this out-of-body experience. I was now eager to finish the interaction that had begun so long ago; there was something I had missed and I wanted to find out what it was.

The closest I can come to describing what I was feeling is the joy of experiencing music, only multiplied a million times over, with nothing between you and forever. Star formations, black holes, thousands upon thousands of galaxies, colors with no names, sounds, tones like the largest pipe organ you will ever hear, it went on with no limit. Everything is resonant and harmonized and seems to work perfectly together, although not in the way you would expect. It is the blending of creation born of chaos.

No sooner had I thought of finishing the meeting with 'that person', than immediately I again shifted perspective. I was now hanging above a planet in a solar system very far away. It looked like Jupiter, huge, red, gas-covered, rotating slowly and majestically around a fiery sun, hanging in space, although I knew somehow that it was a million galaxies away from here. The backdrop of stars on blue velvet hung behind it, but the constellations were completely different from the ones we know here.

Up to now, I had perceived myself as looking like I do now, a woman from Earth, small, but still human in form. Now, instead of this woman, I was pure energy, a huge ball of white light edged in gold, and I realized that it was my true nature. To be your true essence is like no other feeling, it's like coming home. Another ball of white light hung near me. Again, this tremendous level of loving energy flooded me, merging us together. This time I recognized immediately who it was and didn't fight it. We merged into two personalities with one consciousness.

Then immediately like lightning striking, I got it. I started laughing, and he laughed with me. All That Is sparkled and danced at the sound.

'You get it now, don't you?' He said.

'Yes. I get it now.'

Years ago, in the forties, there was a comic strip called Pogo, about a little fox-like creature who was environmentally conscious long before it was fashionable. In one strip, Pogo took a famous quote from a World War I general and turned it around for his own purposes. The general had said it after winning a battle, the name and the general now long forgotten. What he said was "We have seen the enemy, and we have won." In an ironic twist of words, Pogo, referring to our misuse of the Earth and its resources, said, " We have seen the enemy and it is us." What came to me was the reason for our existence, why and where God is, all of this. I was laughing now because it was so obvious; it's right in front of our noses.

'I have seen divinity, and it is us.' I replied, I could hardly even think, I was laughing so hard. Tears of laughter flew off like sparks. There was no difference; him, us, everything, it was all the same, and all of this, this magnificent, real illusion, had been created solely for us.

His energy sobered down, and he became serious.

'You have to go back, you know.'

'I don't want to go.' I have never said anything so heartfelt in my whole life. This was where my true nature lives, where we all live. I thought about what he was asking me to do.

'You promised.'

'I know.' Somehow I knew that I had made that promise. Later when I looked back on it, I realized that I had really been given a choice as to whether I wanted to come back, so the closest description to this vision would be of sort of a near-death experience.

My perspective never quite went back to the way it was before, although there's always more work to do. I don't think we're ever done if we're still here. But this is the question, this is it, the canvas we've been given, to create, to love, to be here now, to find out that the reflection in the mirror is really us. Are you there in your life? It's for you.

Healer, Heal Thyself

So what happened to me, I can hear you asking? Well, after reading this book, from your point of view, either I went off the deep end or I turned out all right. I'm sitting here writing, alive and well, so some part of it must have turned out OK. After I finished my research on Reiki at the University of Michigan, I moved to England to continue working in medical research with my mentor and primary investigator, a physician who is truly a healer himself. I then returned to the States, to the Midwest, where I completed my PhD in Human Development and continue to do research. My life has always been an adventure, so it seems fitting. As you could probably tell, I always have to know what's on the other side of the mountain, no matter what it is.

I haven't focused much on the war stories that always accompany a person in recovery from drug and alcohol addiction. We all have them, and they don't differ much from person to person. And while the experiences I have talked about here may be a little off the beaten track and have given me an unusual perspective in many ways, I still have to deal with all of the things that everyone has to deal with, loss of faith, disappointments, the burdens in life that everyone faces. There are moments of illumination, certainly, but it's as hard for me to remember what I've learned as it is for everyone else.

Much of this book has dealt with individuals who made a conscious, or sometimes not so conscious, decision to leave this plane and go to the next one. But it hasn't dealt much with the decisions we all have to make to live. After working with other addicts and alcoholics as well as the dying, there is one thing that has become very clear to me. All of us, every single one of us is given this choice at some point or another. It may not be as clear as when faced with cancer or bottoming out from an addiction; sometimes that moment comes very quietly, but it always comes. When faced with that fire-breathing dragon we crammed in the back of the darkest room in the deepest place we know inside of us, we hope that no one will ever find it. There's only one problem with that: we know where the dragon lives, and it's only a matter of time before he breaks free of his bonds and comes leaping out of his closet into the light of day.

There are many ways of evading the question All That Is has for us: do we want to be here or not? Alcoholism and drug abuse are several ways of avoiding the question, but as those of us who have tried them know, they do not work, because eventually they will destroy you. But those are really the most obvious of temporary solutions. As we have seen here, there are a myriad of other ways not to face who we are. Insanity is another way, but because that's a universe of our own construction made up of only the things we know, we end up running around in circles, doing the same things over and over again, and learning nothing. We all live in a world of illusion to a greater or lesser degree, no one sees the world exactly as it is. Still, we all have things of which we are most afraid. Most of us spend our lives trying to deny our dragons, but they breathe fire for a reason.

The Buddhists have a saying, *"Before enlightenment, chop wood, carry water, after enlightenment, chop wood, carry water."* Some of the most useful lessons I have learned were revealed sitting at a stop light in traffic, easily as illuminating as hanging out in space and relating to the Cosmos. Sometimes the lessons come easily, and sometimes after much pain, repeatedly doing things that don't work, but everyone has a connection to where the truth is, and that's where the answer lies. That's what makes these experiences different from insanity; they don't come from losing your mind, they come from losing your ego, and you never know you're there until everything else has burned away. All that's left at that point is you and the dragon, and now he has a name.

So it was with the story of Susan, whose death happened early in my healing career. I did not know what to do with her story, and yet, I knew I was supposed to include it. Susan's passing did not seem terribly hopeful at the time, it just seemed to make no sense. Every time I began to write her story down I ground to a halt, and I couldn't figure out why, it was maddening. Her's was a life of grays and black, and she went into the dark by herself. My biggest regret with Susan was that I had not been able to do more to help her. But then she didn't let me; she didn't want me to.

Susan was the older sister of a friend, Michael. When I met her she was dying of the effects of an inoperable benign pelvic mass. Even benign masses can kill you if they're big enough. This one was crushing her internal organs. She was 47 years old.

Susan was a social scientist, a statistician. She was the eldest of three children, in addition to my friend, Michael, there was also a younger sister. Susan had a pleasant face, ash-brown hair and blue eyes, but she looked much older than her age. Looking at her, I knew she would have looked older even without having endured chemotherapy. It was clear she had gone through a lot in her life. Susan had never married, she wore tweeds and sensible shoes and lived alone with her cats, the proverbial spinster.

Her childhood had been chaotic to say the least. Both of her parents were practicing alcoholics as were both of her siblings, although they had gotten into recovery as adults; that's where I met Michael. Susan also drank a lot, although being bedridden limited her consumption to a great degree, she still managed to get it from somewhere. At this point it didn't really matter if she was addicted anyway. Susan was dying.

Toward the end of her illness, Susan had occasional fits of rage where she would scream and throw anything within reach. These fits were not directed at anyone in particular; they were just sort of storms of rage about her situation. No one could blame her, I certainly couldn't. What had been the point of all she was going through? Throughout their lives, her father had been an emotional terrorist to Susan and her siblings. To this day, Michael cannot bring up the topic of his elder sister without choking up. For years, their father had abused them for no other reason other than the sheer pleasure of torturing beings weaker than himself. Some people do the best they can as parents, some do not, he was decidedly a member of the latter group. As I got to know her better, it became clear to me that as the eldest, Susan had taken the brunt of her father's brutality. Michael told me later that he was convinced their father had, in essence, emotionally tortured Susan to death. I know it's hard for some people to encompass this idea, that parents can systematically torture their kids over a lifetime, but there it is. What little he had, he had bequeathed to his children, he was an alcoholic, and with his abuse, his children had inherited the disease.

When I met her, Susan looked like a prisoner of war camp victim. You could have placed her behind a barbed wire fence and it would have looked like a photo from Auschwitz. In a way, this was a good metaphor for Susan, everything had been denied her, even her life. Upon being told of her terminal diagnosis, she had moved out of her home, given away most of her belongings and found homes for her cats. She also moved to an apartment closer to the hospital where she was being treated. Susan spent her last days in a motorized hospital bed, surrounded by boxes she had packed and labeled for the Salvation Army.

I was astounded. What kind of person could think in such practical terms when they were dying? What must Susan think of herself to send away the creatures with which she had the strongest emotional connections, the only real connections to in this life, particularly when she needed them the most? What could have happened to you to think that treating yourself this way was acceptable? Then the answer came to me; Susan really had no connection with any living person, and certainly not with herself, so why should she treat herself any better than she did? She didn't feel she deserved it.

I was only able to work with her for about a month before she died, so there really wasn't much time to get to know her well. Susan was very pragmatic, surely, but not cold, she was kind to everyone. Her employers thought the world of her. She was unbelievably brave, even facing what she thought was oblivion. Susan was an atheist and didn't believe that anything existed after this life. She hadn't believed a bit of it when I told her about other experiences I had observed with other people when they had transitioned. She didn't believe it either when I told her how much I admired her and had even come to love her in a very short time. I couldn't help it; her life had been spent giving to others. But she really couldn't accept any of it.

Although she said differently at first, Susan did not really want to live. She had gone through enough, and rather than tell her father to go to hell, she had chosen to leave instead. Her decision wasn't as proactive as jumping off a bridge or shooting herself, but it was just as effective and suited her self-image of deserving no better. We had this discussion on one of her last days alive. The light of truth was in her eyes when she told me this.

As I've mentioned, I think this happens a lot, you can see it coming. A married couple whose only connection is a venomous rage over 50 years, although they don't have the courage to divorce. Yet one or both die of cancer within a short period of each other. It was a lifelong battle and they both won, or lost, depending on your point of view. I have watched whole families of siblings die young because the parents, after losing a child, decided consciously not to love the others, it was too hard for them to commit themselves again. Was it commonly inherited genes that all of these children died of heart or lung problems in their forties? Perhaps. But familial emotional models are also passed down, I think. The heart energy center is the one most affected by lack of love, I have seen it too many times not to notice the connection. In Susan's case, 47 years of hatred, or just plain being ignored, was so big and ugly I could feel it as soon as I walked in the room, and it had to go somewhere. When we take what's given to us and don't let go of it, love or hate, we can thrive on it, or we can die from it.

Many of our sessions together were simply me listening to her talk. When it became clear that this was what she really wanted to do, who was I to disagree with her? Susan had been through enough in her life and she was done. She was in no physical pain, she had been connected to a morphine pump weeks before we met. She was brave and honest enough to see what she was doing, and to walk through that door unafraid. So I felt the best I could do was support her, to honor Susan's decision and let her go. When she finally passed, it was a relief to everyone, including Susan. Michael told me that, upon informing their father, he scoffed about it for a moment and then went back to talking about the local university football game. Certainly much blame for his psychopathy, for he was a psychopath, might be assigned to how he was brought up, but at some point or another, each of us has to take responsibility for our own behavior. If there are other lives that we live and such a thing as karma, then he's got a lot of backwash to clean up.

As I said earlier, every time I had tried to write Susan's story in the past, there was always something there that had stopped me; it always made me very uncomfortable. Finally, I realized that, in many ways, Susan and I were very alike. Both of us were in research, both of us rather emotionally isolated, and for many of the same reasons. I had been through some hard things too, no less hard than hers. My mother had treated her children much the same way Susan's father treated his. I thought I had already worked through all of that, but had I, really? Susan had held herself away from life, not allowing herself to be loved, even by her cats at the end. Had I done that? Seeing oneself in the mirror is not always comfortable.

One night, after having thrown the story out for what I thought was the last time, I went out with a friend for Chinese food. This was a particularly good restaurant, but more importantly in this case, I loved their fortune cookies; they always had great fortunes in them. My friend knew of my current struggle, so we ate dinner without speaking of it, still, Susan was very heavy on my mind. At the end of dinner I cracked open my fortune cookie. It said, "How can you have a beautiful ending without making beautiful mistakes?" I burst out laughing, I knew it was from Susan, *'Don't do what I did,'* I heard her say. I could feel her laughing. Sometimes winning feels like losing at first, until you get what it was about.

She had chosen to leave and I had chosen to stay. There had been times struggling in recovery when I had come very close to choosing to leave here as well, we all know there is much ugliness in the world. But I know now there has been so much that I would have missed, the loveliness of this place we call home, my friends, the music that I love so much. But more important than the simple physical things, I now understand that we are all integrally connected to each other, this is where our greatest strength lies. It's when you get that you're a human being after all, with all of the warts as well as the luminosity that comes with that title, and realizing that everyone has them. Did Susan's father deserve forgiveness? Perhaps he did, and perhaps not, that isn't up to us to decide. But Susan did, of herself, so she could truly see what was hers by divine right.

Some lessons are only learned in groups of two or more, this I know now. Knowing that love is actually the greater power and is what really feeds us, and that we all deserve it, is a lesson that not all of us get. But I know, even having learned all this, that there are still times when the things asked of us are far more arduous than we were ever told, or even imagined. None of us are exempt.

Small acts of courage make up the bulk of this life. Not the big barnburners where the bacon was saved and the fortune made, but the little stuff, like getting up in the morning when you know it's going to be a disaster today. And you never know, sometimes it turns out better than you think. You're still here, aren't you? Well, so am I. Welcome to the club.

James

The little boy stood at the end of the hospital bed, holding his younger brothers' hands as they stood with their father. Little Cornelius, Connie, on the one side and John Joseph, Joe, on the other. They were in a state run psychiatric ward, but James had no way of knowing that. His father, a handsome man with large blue eyes and a shock of black hair stood beside them, looking down at the motionless inhabitant of the cast-iron bed. A man in a white coat stood near the head of the bed, with a calm and serious, but rather sad look on his face.

'Has she made no sign?' said his father with a heavy Irish brogue.

'No, not in the eighteen months she's been here. We've tried everything, shock therapy, hydrotherapy, drugs, nothing seems to have made any significant effect. She remains as you see her.' The young woman in the bed was completely frozen, staring up unblinking at the ceiling.

His father had told James that the woman was his mother, but this was a far cry from the woman he now only vaguely remembered, the memory felt far away. He looked down at his brothers. Connie was impatiently tugging his hand to go play and Joe had just plopped down on the cement floor with a stuffed toy that James had brought along to keep him occupied. Joe's face was lit up by the sun coming through the window, it highlighted the large portwine birthmark on his face. Older Connie's pageboy hair gleamed jet-black, just like his father's, his eyes blue and round.

'Has she responded to you at all while you've been here?' said the doctor.

"Nah, not a bit," his father replied.

'Have you put the children up to talk to her?'

'Yea, nothing.' The father looked pale and bent from fatigue.

'When did this start?' asked the doctor, curiously.

'Yea, it was just after the youngest was born.' He pointed to Joe sitting on the floor with his rag toy.

'The mark on his face broke her heart, I think. She couldn't fathom it. Nothing like that has happened in her family, or mine.' They both looked at the little boy on floor, handsome and lively, the mark bisecting his face like a harlequin's mask.

'It's been a hard road without her. I've had to give them up to the county a couple of times. It's been too much.'

James had lived with a number of different couples, sometimes with his brothers, Connie and Joe, sometimes not. To be away from them worried him terribly. It was always a relief when their Dad came to get them again, although it meant that James had to get his brothers up early to get ready for the babysitter, their great-aunt when she could take them, and get himself to school in the morning.

'I'll be putting this one out to work soon,' the father said, pointing to James, whose ears perked up at these words. 'He's near ten. I do not want to, but I don't make enough to take care of them.' James wanted to help out, but who would take care of his brothers while he was working?

The woman in the bed made no sign, a prone statue in bed clothes, inert. The doctor sighed. 'Well, perhaps she will change someday. We don't really know any more about this illness than we did a hundred years ago. Keep bringing the boys by now and then; perhaps it will shock her enough to bring her back.'

"I cannot come often,' the father said, "I'm a baker, and I work early in the morning.' He looked at the woman again, although only thirty years old, she could have passed for fifty. His muscles in his jaw tensed and he looked away.

'Well, do what you can. I wish there was more I could tell you. It was nice to meet you, sir.' The doctor shook his hand, picked up his clipboard and left the room, already focused on his next patient.

His father took one last look at the mute body in the bed, gathered up his children and turned away. James couldn't see his face but his father's posture and movements were stiff. He and his brothers never saw their mother again.

James never married. Talking to people was difficult for him; he had been put out to foster care so many times or worked in situations where he was better off not talking, so it was tough to develop a relationship with anyone. Best off just keeping your head down and getting on with the task at hand. He loved numbers, and the machines at the manufacturing jobs he had worked delighted him, so when he was old enough, he entered college and got his engineering degree. Connie shared James' love of numbers and became an accountant. Joe, however, had rebelled against the drudgery of the Great Depression and became an acrobat in the circus. When the Japanese bombed Pearl Harbor, all of them enlisted in the Army. Connie ended up in the Philippines, Joe in the Battle of the Bulge, while James remained stateside, much to his frustration.

He developed a talent for drawing. It was therapeutic for him, he filled pad after pad of paper with drawings of his daily life from childhood, working in manufacturing, precise schematics of boats and trains. But he also drew portraits, he had a unique ability to capture the essence of whomever he was sketching. His best were of Sitting Bull and Mark Twain, these sketches were eerie in their likeness to the originals.

Many of the characters' faces he drew were basic and expressionless, except for one tiny cameo, carefully drawn in pencil, of a young woman, courted by an ardent suitor. Her face was pretty, her dress in the style of the late 1930's, slender with a wide collar. The young man trying to get her attention looked familiar, he was presenting her with a dozen roses and a box of chocolates. The girl was seated before him, her head encircled with dream bubbles of handsome leading men she was considering, and completely ignoring the young man with the flowers.

Of course, the young man had been James, and the girl was the only one he had ever fallen in love with. Never again did another like her come into his life. All that was left was the carefully detailed picture.

· · · ·

When James was 62, he was out driving, a man stepped out in front of his car. James couldn't avoid him, and he hit the man, killing him. The police ruled that James was not at fault, but James took it to heart, spiraling down into a severe depression, fueled by delusions of guilt. Connie, who was my father, then had committed him to a mental hospital.

At the time, I thought that was the end, James would follow in his mother's footsteps and languish in that state until his death. Not so, James proved to be made of a tougher fabric, I should have known from his history that he would get better, and he did, albeit gradually. He made a complete turnaround.

We had not always gotten along well. At the time of my father's death, James had been living with him, as my father's executor, I made some decisions that James did not agree with. We nearly come to blows over paying for my father's funeral expenses. For thirty years, then, since my father's passing, our relationship had been strained. He was the type with whom broken ties were hard to mend. Being gregarious and energetic, and female, I was the type of person who made him anxious. But when I came back from England, I took over the management of his care, paying his bills and making sure he had what he needed; as a result our relationship softened and became less arduous over time.

As he approached his late nineties, he seemed determined to make it to 100 years old; being a retired engineer, he approached his goal in a very systematic way. He exercised, did not allow himself to get fat, and hated TV. He read constantly; he was reading Ayn Rand's *Atlas Shrugged* at the time of his death, and ushered at his church. And of course, he continued to draw. He was a gentle, sweet soul, any direct remarks he made about anything were softened into an absolute truth that you couldn't argue with. One day when we were watching some sort of action thriller, rife with explosions and car chases, put into the DVD player by one of the care assistants. The other inhabitants of the house were stationed in front of the TV like statues, the two of us were the only ones aware of what was going on.

He told me that he wasn't sure, but he thought this might be a stupid movie. I laughed and told him, yes, he was exactly right, it was a very stupid movie. Such a reaction was typical of Uncle James, he gently ignored anything that condescended to his active and questioning mind.

How we interacted when shopping for clothes typified how our relationship had evolved. The task had evolved into sort of a game for us. He was very small, so I had to shop in the boy's department for his clothes. He was also very picky, and very little I selected ever seemed to work right for him. I couldn't blame him, he wanted what he wanted, and I had no objection, I enjoyed spoiling him, he had earned it. I used to search all over town, but whatever I bought would almost always end up being donated to thrift stores. We got to the point where we would laugh about it; I'd show up at his care home and he'd be wearing rags from ten years ago. It was nearly impossible to find clothes that worked for him.

Our relationship continued to get better, now he just chirped constantly about everything when we were together. Engineering, his jobs as a boy long ago, his church activities, It had taken a while, but he was finally relaxed enough to consider me a friend. For his 100th birthday, his church had celebration; more than 100 people attended the party. The children from the parish school came too, they wanted to touch someone 100 years old and listen to his stories of living through the Great Depression. It turned out to be his last hurrah. Even with all of my experience and gained knowledge, I dreaded the coming loss of my friend.

About six months after his centenary celebration, his congestive heart failure worsened, and he started to complain of shortness of breath. His care home nurse took him to the hospital and he was admitted as an inpatient. He had experienced shortness of breath before, but this time I knew it was different. I had been tipped off, so I anxiously flew back to be with him.

A month before he was admitted to the hospital, I had been with him to handle some of his financial affairs, when a peculiar conversation between us ensued. There were times he could be a little fuzzy mentally, so he again went over what he wanted done with his remains. That is not what put me on guard. We were sitting in the cluttered little corner he carved out of his bedroom for an office, amidst his books and drawings, with the afternoon sun coming in the windows. It was a beautiful early spring day. As we looked out the window, he made the only pensive remark I have ever heard him make about his childhood.

'My childhood was not the happiest, but I've learned that you must remain positive. You have a choice, and you make it what it is. Is there anything you want to ask me?' I was amazed at his candor, he had never made remarks like this before. I replied after a moment of thought. I took the opportunity to ask about the family mystery, his mother.

'Yes, yes, I do. What do you remember of your mother, my grandmother, Bridget?' He answered me without qualm or self-pity.

'I only really remember seeing her once in the hospital. She was lying in a bed, staring up at the ceiling. She didn't recognize me.' I felt quietly sad thinking about three little boys and their forlorn father standing at her bedside, hoping that something, anything, would bring her back to them. Nothing ever did. She died 70 years later, still in the psychiatric ward. The conversation meandered a little, but then another warning surfaced.

'Well, Uncle James, I have to go now, I'll see you soon.' I gave him a hug, as I usually did.

'Goodbye,' he said. My radar had been pinging at the curious turn of the conversation, it seemed very "final," but now it rang like a firebell. He had never said goodbye before; it was always 'So long,' or 'Ok,' things like that. Not long now, I thought. I left knowing I would be back soon.

Sure enough, in two weeks, I was called back; he was worse. His personal health care assistant, Ed, a little Filipino man, had an interesting story for me when I arrived at the care home.

He said that James had not been sleeping very well, and had talked a lot in his sleep during the previous two weeks. James told him, half-awake, that there were people coming though the ceiling to "take him home." The literature actually supports this experience; as many as 90% of patients dying in intensive care units experience visions of their relatives in spirit before passing. I knew then I had made the right call in coming back immediately; the signs I had learned to recognize were all there.

I was determined that this time would be different from my father's passing, it would be exactly the way my uncle wanted it. The promise I made decades ago came back to me, that I would make this process better if it were within my power to do so. This time I felt I was ready but, like a runner who has trained and studied but has not yet approached the starting line. I wouldn't know until we were in it.

James and I had signed a medical power of attorney together; I would have the power to make his medical decisions should he be unable to do so. Without the next-of-kin possessing power of attorney in medical decision-making, the medical team then bears the burden, and they don't want it. James wished for no extraordinary measures to be taken and I was here to honor that.

My phone beeped with a message from his attending physician as soon as my plane landed. My uncle had slipped out of consciousness as soon as he was admitted, his doctor was puzzled. I asked him to just make him as comfortable as possible; James was resisting his vital signs being taken and had refused an ultrasound by crossing his arms in front of his chest. The road before us was now clearly laid out; he had turned his face away and was now looking someplace else. It was now time to bring all of what I had learned to bear.

When I entered his room, it was quiet, and there was a music channel playing softly on the TV. I spoke to him, to let him know I was there. Outside were a few California eucalyptus trees, with their long, silver leaves and pungent smell coming through the slightly open window. His room was on the corner and had windows on both sides, a light-filled, airy space.

He was breathing slowly but regularly, his color and energy looked fairly normal but weakened in tiny, almost imperceptible ways. He seemed internally directed and not focused on the outer world at all. I let him know immediately that we would be doing nothing that we hadn't talked about, and that no extraordinary measures would be taken.

I was sad that he was leaving, but I had to remain focused on the fact that this was his process, not mine. I could see that his attention was peripherally focused on me for the moment, so I filled him in on what I was doing, where I was working, other small details of my life. Sometimes the small conversations are just as important as the big ones.

I realized that I was proud to have come from such a line, despite our flaws. His strength of will had been indomitable. Everyone around him loved him. He had overcome so much, his childhood, the Great Depression, service in World War II, his accident, his own personal battles, and had done it with great strength and bravery. Courage is everywhere, you just have to look for it. We had traveled the last part of the road together. We had made peace at last; it was just the two of us.

The first day went quietly, I read and spoke to him intermittently. His energy was fading, but his color was still pink. His doctor came in and said he was puzzled; he couldn't figure out why James wasn't conscious or speaking. It occurred to me, I knew exactly what was going on, my Dad left when he meant to, and so would James. I told the doctor that as a family, we are very strong-willed, and that we decide when we leave, and that it wouldn't be long.

The hospital staff had wheeled a bed into his room so I could sleep there with him at night. The medical staff immediately ceded decision-making power to me and offered palliative care services. The difference between this scenario and the one with my father was like black and white. Where thirty years ago it was an arduous uphill climb, full of labyrinths and dark spaces, this one was an easy, peaceful road.

I called Ed and asked him to come. He and my uncle had been very close; they were alike in many ways. Both small and quiet, and bachelors for life, they had developed a strong affinity for each other. Because of the general inertness of his fellow inhabitants in the care home, James didn't really speak to anyone but Ed. They were good friends. My uncle did not rouse or speak when Ed arrived, but I could tell that James' attention was focused on Ed when he entered the room.

Ed moved up close to the side of the bed, where James was lying motionless, and told him in a joking way that waffles were ready. James was a good eater, and his favorite food was waffles. Something near a smile broke out over James' face, and his eyes, which were only partially closed, twinkled as he focused blearily at Ed for a moment, I could tell he was silently laughing. We all laughed together, comfortably, it was a good moment.

On the second day I had hurriedly gone to check in at my hotel, but when I returned just a few hours later, I was struck by the radical change, James' appearance and energy had faded markedly. He was now very pale and waxen, and his breathing had become spasmodic. A thought came to my mind; my uncle was a very private man, did he want to be alone to do this? Some people do, my father had died alone. Even years later, I think he preferred it that way. But James seemed to be waiting for something else, he had an air of expectancy around him. Nervous, I thought I was going to miss a sign.

I began to prepare the room by meditating and praying. All of the spiritual paths indicate in their various texts that the space where the dying person is should be held quiet and as a sacred space for the person to do the work of transition, I wanted a good space to be ready for him.

I focused on calm and asked for all of his guides and relatives to be present, as I had done so many times before. The room's energy was starting to feel full, I knew I was not alone. I said aloud, 'Where are you?' and at that moment a camera flash occurred in a corner of the room. I heard words in my head, *'Don't worry, we're here with you.'* A white shadow sparkled and shimmered at the corner of the bed on the other side. I could see a flash of black hair and those large blue eyes. It was my grandfather. I relaxed a bit, but I was still stressed, what was James waiting for? There was something I was still missing; what was it?

When I returned from grabbing a quick bite, his parish priest was in the room conducting Last Rites. James was fiercely Catholic, and very devout. I had put off contacting the priest; as I mentioned, I'm a sort of lapsed Catholic. Last Rites in Catholicism ask for forgiveness for the dying person, and I'm always reminded of the quote, made by Henry David Thoreau, as he approached death. When asked by an aunt if he had made his peace with God, he replied, 'I didn't know we had quarreled.' James was possibly one of the sweetest, kindest people I had ever known, in my view he no sooner had to ask forgiveness for anything than fly to the moon.

But here's where I had made a mistake. I had qualms as we proceeded into this process; but as we stood in a circle around him and prayed, I watched my uncle's body relax; here was the thing he had been waiting for. I had forgotten, rituals are important to us and give us meaning. That he thought he needed forgiveness was inexplicable to me, but I was again reminded that this was not my journey.

As the sun paced out the sky that day, his physical changes started accelerating. James' energy was becoming dimmer and more submerged. His blood pressure dropped so low as to not be detectable; his organ systems were shutting down. The sunset through the windows shone fierce and golden on his face, waxed and waned, then darkening into soft twilight as our journey together progressed.

The lights in the hallway had been dimmed by the nurses, to encourage the patients to sleep. A circle of quiet peace enveloped us, and the familiar whispers and rustles became more discernable, they were gathering around him in spirit. I had a small light turned on so I could read, and to keep a watchful eye over him. But I was still concerned, it continued to run around my mind, did he want me to give him more privacy or stay here? I was getting no sign and I couldn't bring myself to leave.

· · · ·

The tiny old man lay on the bed, the room around him becoming dimmer and dimmer. He knew he was in a hospital, and that a priest had come in the room earlier and said some things. He couldn't really remember what they were, but he remembered that he felt more at peace after the priest's visit. There was a woman sitting next to the bed with black hair, and although her eyes were brown —he knew that from long history—her eyes reminded him of his brother. He couldn't really grasp her name though. He knew it once, but not anymore. There was a connection between them, this he remembered, but he couldn't recall exactly what that was either. It didn't matter.

There were outlines in the room, and rustles and whispers that hinted at voices, but he couldn't make out who they were or what they were saying. That old frame was fading, and the new one becoming more real.

A young man in burgundy scrubs came into the hospital room, working the night shift. He was young, with a shock of red hair. He asked if the patient was going to get a treatment. The woman with dark hair, comfortably sitting and reading a book next to the bed, responded with a smile. The old man could see her through the haze of half-closed eyes.

'No, that order was discontinued. It probably just hasn't been written up in his medical record yet. He is choosing to leave now, so there is no need for respiratory therapy.'

'Oh, I am so sorry, I didn't mean to intrude,' said the young man. He looked pained.

'You're not intruding, you just didn't know.' The young man looked at the woman curiously; medical personnel are used to family members being stressed about their loved one's impending death.

'I know my family pretty well, we decide when we leave. From my experience, most people do choose when they leave, actually.' The old man was pleased; she understood. It had been a long life, the door was approaching.

Intrigued, the young man advanced into the room; he had never heard anyone talk like this, not the doctors and nurses, no one. It was slow and there was not much going on, so when the woman invited him to sit down, he pulled up a chair. The old man's breathing was becoming less frequent, more spasmodic.

'They leave when they want to?' His query was artless and not argumentative. He looked like a flame in the darkening room with the sun striking him through the windows, the rest of the room blue and grey.

'I can't say this applies to everyone, but it seems that a decision to leave is made at some point and some level.'

'How do you deal with it when the patient asks how they're doing? Even the docs seem to have a hard time with this. I know I do.'

'It really isn't our process, is it? It's theirs. Your best approach is to turn it back to them. Ask them how they think they're doing. Usually when given a window, they know how they're doing and want to talk about it.' He considered that for a moment.

'But what if they don't die soon? Isn't that just upsetting the family?'

'Sometimes they don't die when they think they will—or they pull back for a moment, I think, from fear. It's a process every patient goes through step-by-step.'

'Sometimes I don't know what to say. The family hangs on, sometimes they are so frantic.'

'Well, to some degree, it's their process too. But it helps to remind them that their loved one needs them to be accepting as much as they can. Otherwise they can hang on after the patient is ready to leave. But sometimes that's the best they can do. Not everyone can resolve issues remaining from an entire lifetime with the dying person, it's too big. But if you can encourage them to forgive themselves and their loved one, that's the biggest thing, I think.'

The woman's voice was getting farther and farther away, and the room was becoming lighter and lighter, despite that dusk had filled the room. Figures were becoming clearer and more distinct, voices were calling him. His father, mother and brothers were there before him. As the woman spoke to the young man, James quietly stepped out.

• • • •

When the young man left the room, I turned back to James. He had made no sign, no rasping last breath, but his old body was now empty. Now I knew what he had wanted. He had waited for me to be distracted, to give him a little space. He had passed away at exactly 100 years, six months old. I cried in relief, it was like him to be so precise. The ends of the circle had met at last.

For All of Us

We will all face death one day, and we will all probably be witness to the same process in others as well, it's part of who we are. When it's your own family member, the process can be very difficult, and a strong support system may be the best we can do to get through it. Often, we are too close to the situation to be of any help, we need help ourselves.

Some people do well by discussing it, others go to that door with little or no discussion at all. There are no hard and fast rules, everyone goes through this final act in their own way. But allow me to say one thing to you before going on. You are not being selfish by feeling anger at this process, nor am I going to tell you that it will get better with time. You are going to miss them physically, and if you are reading this, you're probably at the stage of just wanting this not to happen, or if it has already, you just want them back. You just want them back. That's OK, and perfectly normal. You are not being selfish. It's called love and right now it hurts.

But if you're paying attention, there are signs that the process might be progressing in a manner that family members and even the medical professional might not be aware of. Every effort, of course, should be made to maintain adequate and appropriate pain control; fortunately knowledge has progressed in this regard to the level of a fine art since my father passed away. No person should have to experience the kind of pain that robs us of our ability to die with respect.

But even when this can't be achieved, any discussion the person is willing to participate in can help reduce their fears. Sometimes this cannot be accomplished by another family member; here is where the professional caregiver can work wonders. One of the most effective things you can do is ask the person how *they think they are doing.* Medical professionals are people too, and face the same fears the rest of us do, too often they are willing to tell the patient how they think the patient is faring to try and make it OK, which can overwhelm the patient into silence. Patients know far more than we give them credit for and they need to be acknowledged and heard.

Never forget that the patient can hear you when you speak, even when they are unconscious. I have witnessed this more times than I can count; caregivers assume or at least forget that the patient's lack of responsiveness doesn't mean they lack consciousness and awareness of their surroundings. I assume at all times that the patient can hear me and, even in extreme cases of brain damage such as Madelyn, are aware at some other level of what is going on around them.

I am not going to get into other energetic processes observed in Buddhist texts, the majority of these are minute changes that only individuals practiced in identifying these techniques can actually perceive. They don't have much bearing on the average situation in the Western perspective, but they are certainly worth reading if you are interested, the references are in the back of this book.

But some of these energetic processes do seem to be associated with physiological and psychological changes that can be used as benchmarks for impending transition. What I've found remarkable is that, like the birth process, almost all of these stages, with the exception of the energy's actual exit from the body, can be stopped and even reversed, and frequently are stopped unconsciously by the patient. As I have said, our intention drives us, and most often the fear of the actual moment of death, or waiting for someone to come say goodbye are among the reasons dying processes are temporarily reversed.

The most common sign of impending death is when the temperature of the extremities drops to the point of feeling ice-cold to the touch. This is a preliminary sign and very easily can be turned back. But this always marks the beginning of the process. This correlates with the exiting of the "winds" in Buddhist literature, another word, a metaphor, for physiological energy. It makes sense that as the body's energy diminishes, so does the body temperature.

Just prior to transition, the heart and respiratory rate in all cases I have observed becomes irregular and spasmodic. At the very end, the respiratory rate drops down to two to four breaths per minute and the heart rate down to the 20s and 30s. This is a stronger, more immediate sign than losing body temperature, although I have seen patients pull back from this one as well. Loss of body temperature can occur weeks ahead of transition, or just prior to it. Slowing heart rate and respiration usually means that transition is closer, just usually days, perhaps a week at most, and again, sometimes just prior to passing.

A different process that many people find uncomfortable is the patient sometimes seeing or talking to people who have already passed over. Persuasive argument could be made for both sides of the issue, that brain function is deteriorating, the patient is losing contact with reality and is hallucinating, or that this is the beginning of the next reality. The current literature supports the observation that many people in hospice have similar experiences—seeing and talking to loved ones who have already passed. My feeling is to let them be, unless it seems to be agitating them too much. We have more control over our surroundings that we realize. The patient can very easily control this phenomenon, by telling the gathered spirits to go away. Sometimes that is all that is necessary. A good rule of thumb to remember is that if they are peaceful visitations, most likely they are real, or at least real to the patient, and are serving a psychological need that the living cannot serve at this time. If the visitations are disturbing, then perhaps thought should be given to administering an anti-anxiety medication.

This touches on another issue, the use of psychotropic medications with the dying. They can be invaluable tools to assist in the comfort of the transitioning patient, but they should be used with the patient's interests in mind. The fact that the relatives are uncomfortable with Dad wanting to talk about dying is not sufficient reason to medicate! Anti-depressants can be useful, particularly when the patient is depressed and having trouble sleeping or eating, and can make them much more comfortable. Keep in mind, when approaching end-stage, eating and drinking are no longer a requirement, so if the dying person refuses, there is really no cause for concern; they are readying themselves for another place.

"Sundowner syndrome," anxiety attacks that occur at the end of the day can be greatly relieved by the use of anti-anxiety medications. None of this should be taken as a mandate; every patient is different and I am not a licensed professional. Each case needs to be assessed on its own merits. When appropriate, the use of these medications can do wonders, and the family is not always in the best emotional shape to consider these very useful tools.

The timing of the last process in death is the hardest to pin down. It can vary, and family members are frequently very puzzled and hurt by it. Though it is an amorphous stage, an energy healer can generally identify it very quickly, because the patient's energy field begins to "loosen" around the patient's body. This is when the patient begins to detach emotionally from this plane and all who live in it. Sometimes this behavior is misidentified resulting in the patient being overmedicated, to attempt to "bring the patient back to reality."

Family members have frequently come to me in tears, hurt and offended, not understanding that this is part of the process. To go "there," the patient must let go of "here." I have seen women in labor get this inward stare as well. It is not that they love you any less, or don't want to talk to you, but they have more pressing matters to focus on right now. At this point it's no longer about you.

Even so, always remember to include yourself in the equation when talking about how to deal with your loved one's transition. Caring for the emotional needs of the transitioning patient can be emotionally harrowing in a health care setting; doing so at home sometimes adds more to the burden. You cannot do this by yourself, nor should you have to. Sometimes we need someone to tell us this in bold print. In the end, you will be the one who suffers the most. Sometimes the unresolved issues between ourselves and the patient can literally drive us crazy; they still know how to press our buttons! One needs to have help and to take breaks, to keep one's energy up over the long term. There are many agencies and hospice care facilities that can assist the family in this process, but you must seek them out.

Remember to grieve, you are not being selfish. You miss them, it's a normal process. It also takes a lot of time to accept, far more time than our culture gives us. I remember watching "Sleepless in Seattle," where the widower, played by Tom Hanks, was admonished by the telephone "therapist" after his wife had only been dead for a year, implying that he was "stuck" in his grief. It takes an average of two years to assimilate and accept a partner's passing, and that is when the grief is processed at an average rate, for many, it takes much longer! But, as is typical of Western culture, those around us are often uncomfortable with anything less than instant gratification, we are not accepting of pain. Life has pain. People who have experienced the passing of a loved one have frequently told me that over time, it's not a thing you "understand," it's just recognized and assimilated into your overall experience of life. It is what it is. Would the highs and lows you have shared with your loved ones be valued as much without the possibility of losing them? I doubt it.

This collection of stories has never been meant as a treatise about religious faith, or to convince anyone that that the "paranormal" exists, to me it is all one matrix. I do know that these types of transpersonal experiences do not hold up to rational analysis. No matter; much of life doesn't hold up to rational analysis. But, as I have frequently joked with my atheist friends, if there really is nothing after this and we cease to exist after death, then we're not going to know or feel it anyway, so what's the problem? Whether or not we exist in the next life, no one can say; we'll all find out when we get there. You can choose whatever you want to believe, whatever seems real to you. The easiest perspective is the existential view, that nothing matters, there is nothing after death. All one has to do is look at the headlines to understand how such a perspective came about, very little seems to make sense at times. But to be overwhelmed by this perspective leads only to temporary fixes, and in the end, continually buying "the next big thing" to induce happiness seems at least counterproductive, if not pointless. Whether you've been given this life accidentally or by some grander design, why not make use of it? It's still for you, a great gift, really. Without the punctuation of death, the song of our lives would have no meaning, no beauty, and no appreciation of the infinite.

I hope, after reading these stories, you may have found something in it for yourself, or perhaps for someone who is at this final door. Understanding is the path to illumination; the more we understand, the less resistance and anxiety we experience, and the dying process, any process really, becomes easier to accept. In the long run, both the Buddha and Jesus may be right, all this is about acceptance and the Light.

For the Seeker

In the classical Western model, medical training to productively interact with dying patients and their families is generally limited to a short elective course in psychiatry or end-of-life issues, unless one specializes in hospice care as a physician. Currently these account for only one in 13,000 physicians in the United States, so there is still a large gap in understanding of the issues surrounding death and dying.

We have progressed, it was enormously gratifying to be offered access to hospice care for my Uncle, given what a struggle it was to care for my dying father so many years ago. Even still, many more deaths occur in Intensive Care Units, one of the biggest moments we will ever face is still overshadowed for the majority by the nervous, pleading cry of 'Fix it and make it go away!'

We need more understanding, but where will we find it? Mainstream Western culture immediately regards events as I have recounted them as impossible and those speaking of them as crazy. Yet I am not the only one able to do or see these things, neither now nor throughout history. If you put these concepts into an historical perspective, they are not as far-fetched as they might seem. In light of this and other questions these stories have brought up, perhaps it would help if we became familiar with some of the work done in the area of caring for the dying and think about them in a trans-disciplinary construct. You can then judge for yourself how these stories might augment our current understanding of this last passage in our lives, and support a larger view of human consciousness.

The Western Perspective

In Western culture, we have a philosophy, a particular ontological view we use to interpret reality that consequently molds our interactions in the world. This philosophy is a result of our culture and history, but it is only one point of view despite our hegemonic belief that it represents the "truth." It is dualistic in nature; I am me, and you are you, that chair is different and separate from this table, and so forth. Nature and technology are two very different horses; the mind is a separate entity from the body. We can be purely objective and define the truth of any given object or event. This perspective was developed almost in backlash to the mindset of the Middle Ages, where Man was the center of the physical universe, and to say differently risked not only ex-communication, but your life. Since that time, how we value knowledge and assess meaning remains essentially rationalist-empirical, Westerners have a strong bias against that which we cannot see and measure. This is changing, but slowly.

Carl Jung's work is most well known in his theory of the collective unconscious, where archetypes and various symbols link possible layers of awareness in unseen communal access to all of us, his ideas being one of the first hints in Western developmental theory of man possessing an expanded consciousness. He wrote extensively about the meaning of death in a spiritual life. Jung had many purported experiences with the collective unconscious as chronicled in his *Red Book*, and believed that the psyche, the spirit of a human being is not subject to the laws of space and time as we currently understand them.

Perceptions of human consciousness in the West did not move forward in much detail past recognition of the level of conformist stage—'If I obey the rules, I will control my environment'—until the first half of the 20th century, when Abraham Maslow changed the focus from the examination of neuroses to human potentials, he began to define those ineffable qualities that fulfill us as human beings. Identifying basic needs that must first be fulfilled, such as food or safety, he went on to prioritize such values as love and self-actualization. He also recognized that transcendence from the purely material plane was possible and had already been accomplished by some individuals. He felt that our final step would be to do so *as a group,* implying a higher dynamic than just individual transcendence was available as a meaningful goal for human evolution. However, he felt that only a few would really achieve it.

But it was not until we get to Stanislav Grof in the Western model of the human psyche that we even begin to acknowledge the existence of a non-corporeal spiritual life and attempt to define a more integral picture of human psychological development. Unfortunately, or perhaps because of this work, depending on your point of view, Grof came to these conclusions by using pharmaceutical LSD to break through neuroses and emotional traumas with volunteers. These altered states, Grof felt, allowed the patient access to emotions and memories that had been repressed as far back as the prenatal period, and bringing them to consciousness allowed the patient to integrate them successfully.

He also recognized that to study the end of life is to understand this life more fully. He also has observed that descriptions of this last process, as recorded in "Books of the Dead" that exist in many cultures shares common characteristics across cultures. He later concluded they may have been simply used as training manuals for the advanced spiritual student, rather than written as exercises in accessing other levels of consciousness, thus deemphasizing their potential as characterizations of the dying process. Grof addressed spirituality within the development of the human spirit while neatly skirting around the presence of an Absolute, but he does come to the conclusion that without an ending, an appreciation of the Now, the transcendent will continue to elude us.

Ken Wilber was really the first Westerner to integrate the development of human consciousness from a evolutionary, cultural and emotional/intellectual and spiritual perspective. His acronym, AQAL, an acronym for All Quadrants, All Levels, is now so ubiquitous that it is recognizable in pop culture, which Wilber addressed in his book, among others, *A Brief History of Everything*. He is a practicing Buddhist, so he follows the Buddhist belief that with death our individual energy returns to the greater energy and is reincarnated in the next life.

Jenny Wade presents a persuasive argument on the possibility of life before and after death in her book, *Changes of Mind, A Holonomic Theory of the Evolution of Consciousness*. As well as looking at various prenatal memories of Grof's volunteers, she points out that all cultures and all times have reported people who have experienced literally thousands of similar near-death experiences. Certainly, it could be said that the brain is "acting out," that is, the ego is devising an explanation of its impending non-existence by hallucinating the creation of an "after-life," but the probability of so many people all creating similar experiences, seems vanishingly small. Merely looking at the statistics regarding reports of near-death experiences, it seems clear that something is happening to the residual energy after the material body dies.

The Eastern Perspective

Many scriptural Buddhist texts describe detailed mechanisms of the death process. They chronicle 100's of years of observations from clairvoyant monks that specialized in the death process about what a person experiences within these stages. There is a cultural overlay evident in these writings, but there are similarities that appear in nearly all death traditions, that the living can direct and safeguard where the dying person's spirit goes by prescribed ritual. Violent or accidental death can upset this process, for example, the ICU ward in the hospital that I wrote about earlier, or the story of Sarah, who didn't know where to go upon leaving her body. There is a story in one of the commentaries of the Tibetan Books of the Dead; a man was walking along a road and was killed instantly by a run-away cart. A passing monk called the man's spirit back into his body momentarily and then, blessing him, directed him to the appropriate next plane of existence, and the man again died. Even in death, despite the crooked and illusory perspective our little minds and egos afford us, we have free will to go where we choose, but sometimes we need help.

Within the Eastern framework, Aurobindo, an Indian psychologist/philosopher specifically focused on human developmental theory, including the continued process of post-death life in the early 20th century. He stated not only that a transcendent level exists, but also that many individuals have already achieved Unity Consciousness through meditation combined with the study of Yoga, calling it the "Supramental" (Super-mind) level. He and his colleague, "The Mother," integrated human development in union with the Absolute as the possible end result of human psychological, spiritual and cognitive evolution. He recognized that this Supramental level accessed levels of information that previously would have been impossible. Progress is made through a process that the soul interacts with thought and action within his or her own understanding, with others, and with "reality" and rebounds continually to a higher plane, until that soul is integrated into Unity with the All.

A key point needs to be made here. Aurobindo, Maslow, Grof, Wilber, and Wade are clear, with some argument, that ours is a nested development and not a linear one. A later stage is dependent on the successful development of a previous stage, and an earlier stage is not capable of grasping a later stage. There is also a great deal of argument as to whether experiences like mine and many others, really, fall into the category of real experience or hallucination as the result of regression to pre-ego formation, which is the central question from our native epistemology that arises from stories such as these. Of course you can see that if they fall into this category, they can be easily dismissed. Here's the issue; the linear, rational/empiricist neurobehaviorally-based perspective brooks no argument by stating the transpersonal view is pathological by definition.

Eastern developmental theory has always assumed that these experiences were the result of study, and that all human beings are neuroanatomically equipped to perceive them, so they are common to all human beings. My own experience has taught me that the mechanism to perceive these things has always been there, as I had transcendent experiences even as a child, but time, experience and study have strengthened their perception and have assigned meaning.

The basic premise that human consciousness not only progresses through cognitive, behavioral and spiritual evolution before and after birth and death partially explains the meaning of these experiences but does not address *why*. But there are other avenues that can be explored.

Shamanic history and experience

Mircea Eliade, in his landmark examination of Shamanic practices around the world, *Shamanism: Techniques of Ecstasy,* describes the practices of accessing altered states of consciousness from within a number of cultures. These practices have a long history, going back to prehistoric Tibet and tracing concurrently to African and Native American indigenous peoples as well as many, many others around the world. There are many cross-cultural similarities, all speaking to cognitive patterns of thought and analysis that were common to all indigenous human beings.

Often its practitioners were recruited by inheritance, ability or initiation by illness or inflicted hardship such as a vision quest, reminiscent of the young doctors and myself. But there is a characteristic that is common to all of them, the information gained through these individuals' access to altered states of consciousness always applies to the survival and evolution of the tribe to a higher level of understanding about their place in the world. Physical and spiritual healings, the performance of ritual and rites of passage, messages from gods and other entities and guidance to the underworld were officiated by the tribal Shaman.

There are many others who are pursuing how this can be accessed such as Michael Harner and Alberto Villoldo, others still who have practiced as shamans in modern times such as Black Elk, and many others still who pursue it on a daily basis either alone or with a teacher or guru. Michael Winkelman, retired from the Arizona State University, has been studying the evolutionary biology of such practice, attempting to identify its organic biological source structures within the brain. His premise is that these structures and their associated functions are hard-wired specifically to access these alternate levels of experience, and that the interpretations of these are the basis of the development of religion. Stanley Krippner, a psychologist at Saybrook University, has also examined these cultural phenomena at length. When you look at accessing altered levels of consciousness as Shamanic journeying with its long history, then these stories become easier to understand as a normal function of human beings.

Carlos Castaneda must be mentioned, if only because his work was the source of such controversy. His investigations, purportedly conducted with the Yaqui Shaman, Don Juan, introduced the concept of non-dual shamanic energywork to the pop consciousness of the late '60s. Castaneda, an anthropologist trained at

UCLA, chronicled his training as a *Nagual*—a medicine man—in the Yaqui Way of Knowledge. After some scrutiny, it was suggested that Castaneda made the whole story up, and that no such person existed by the name of Don Juan. The Yaqui themselves decried the work. Castaneda, to the end of his life, insisted that they were true, and had occurred as he had recorded them.

What does not occur to the scholars—because it can't, really, not within our predominant ontological model—*is that it can be both true and "untrue."* What I mean by "untrue" is that it all may very have occurred as Castaneda described, but just not in this frame of reality. Don Juan may have been a spirit guide of Castaneda's. I have several guides that exist in spirit who could be classified as shamans, one is Andean, and the other North Native American. The teachings that Castaneda received from Don Juan were very similar in basis compared to the training I have received from them. A transpersonal anthropologist, Daniel Noel, was quite skeptical of the source of Castaneda's experiences, but also felt that the stories were still very important for the concepts that they put forward. He noted that the works became popular because they represented the *zeitgeist* of the time and introduced the concept of nondual intentionality manifesting in the real world in a culturally penetrating way. Noel supported an even more important concept; that our psychological model of cognitive and emotional function was sadly bereft of the *imaginal*—Jung's rich world of archetypes from within the collective unconscious. In other words, the beautiful worlds of the human imagination. Even more critical to our mental and emotional health is the recognition of this part of ourselves, and in incorporate it into our daily lives, and in this case, our deaths.

Interestingly, Wilbur considers shamanic work as a "dead end" with his AQAL hypothesis. He believes that their use of tools such as psychotropic drugs made their access to the Absolute only temporary, and their use of them to guide members of the tribe in their daily lives as crude. What this points out is that attaining the Absolute in a permanent manner through meditation is a slightly different endpoint than accessing it as needful for healing and guidance, such as a Shaman might for the benefit of his tribe or group. Whether a vestige of our ancient cultural heritage or a meaningful part of our evolutionary path, our understanding of death remains truncated, a more integrated view as represented may prove relevant. But what is the meaning for us, now, of these types of experiences in our modern society?

Intentionality

In all of these stories, several over-arching themes can be identified. It appears clear that these people who died held prior belief that directed their perception of death. Sarah was descending into the void after leaving her body because that is what she believed would happen. Tom knew on a very deep level he was leaving, so he did. Chris believed that getting into recovery for alcoholism wasn't going to help, and so it didn't. Kevin didn't know that any other way was possible, so the manner in which he died is how it occurred. Alan believed what he saw and made a choice, as did Susan.

But another theme seems to be present as well, that the intervention of another person could change the patient's intention *if they were open to it.* Madelyn, Julie, most notably Sarah, all of their final results were changed as a result of my intention. The little bird didn't know that healing *wasn't* possible, so he did, despite his fatal injuries. This is not to say I am any more powerful than you, the timing was right, and in all cases my intention was driven by compassion, and by remaining open to the possibility of transcendence to a higher level of perception and understanding. This was also true of the young doctors, despite their training and cultural model, they wanted to know more about their experiences from compassion and a wish to help their dying patients, and they were open to change.

The change in a person's intention at the time of passing may be dependent on their thoughts, emotions and overall intention down to their soul level, in addition to direction from a guide. That is, it requires their "permission," surrender, the opening of their energy field to effect a change, which may or may not be a conscious decision, as in the case of Tom. This appears to occur even after death, thereby not requiring a material body to manifest that intention, as in Sarah's case. This core permission does not stay static and can change over time within the same individual. All of the factors that this "change of intention" is dependent upon remain unknown at this time, and may change many times, or not even once in the person's current lifetime. This "change in intention" may be essential to the placebo effect, which has been observed in Western medicine, but has proven frustratingly elusive in terms of mechanism.

The Eastern Framework Revisited

So what precipitates this change in intention? Allow us to go the Eastern perspective once again for a moment. According to the Tibetan Buddhists, there are six bardos that we can experience over the course of our lifetimes. A bardo can be defined roughly as a frame of reference. It's not so much a mood or a mindset, but more how we perceive reality, our ontological foundation. Briefly put, we progress from the life bardo, how we perceive this life in the most attached, material way, to a "neutral resting state" bardo in-between lives, to a "self-examining" bardo, where many of the positive and negative qualities we clung to in this life present themselves for our acceptance or rejection, to an awareness of the pervading illusory quality of this material life. It culminates in the realization of the "Ground of All Being," Nirvana, the Void, or realization and assimilation into the Absolute, the unified Energy of All Things. This occurs after experiencing many lifetimes. With the exception of the "Life bardo," the one in which we are living now, all of these processes occur after death and between lives. Please bear in mind that I am again running roughshod over a large body of literature that describes these bardos in detail, their illumination is exceeded only by their beauty, for much of their teaching involves storytelling of the most descriptive kind. But these are the bare bones of the process.

More specifically, a bardo is a moment of epiphany on a very large scale. Have you ever had one of those "Aha!" moments, when you realized that the world wasn't what you thought it was? Sometimes when this happens, these moments can advance you in large, intuitive steps of understanding from your previous perception of reality. It can also apply to personal day-to-day issues as well, when something, someone or some issue in your life reveals itself in a completely different way. You find it wasn't about *this*, it was about *that*, and what it revealed, you had no idea existed. Your intention, your basic foundational perspective has been forced to the next level of awareness.

The Stages of Elizabeth Kubler-Ross

The psychologist Elizabeth Kubler-Ross delineated a series of processes in her seminal work about the processes that the dying goes through before passing. She identified these stages as denial, anger, bargaining, depression and acceptance. She postulated that while not every person experiences all of these processes—nor do I believe that all do—to resolve these passages successfully, the individual must progress to the level of acceptance. I will add one more aspect, forgiveness, between depression and acceptance. I have witnessed this many times, and for a person to break through to acceptance, there must be forgiveness of themselves and others, and even of God; it is implicit in the process. To break though is a key phrase here, as this is really the same process as that of the bardos, only done while living. Attainment of each level is the shedding, the detachment of another more subtle level of illusion about this life to the realization of the truth, the "Ground of All Being," surrender to and acceptance of the All. One can only look at the process of Julie to understand how far one can come in this process if one is open and fearless. The same seems to be true of Sarah's process and even more significantly, it appeared to occur after her passing.

This epiphanous "change in the nature of mind" is a pivotal moment when that actual matrix upon which the person stands changes in quality and in scope, and is founded on the individual's ability to be open to change. These processes have been identified as the bardos for at least 2500 years and are not limited to Buddhists, as is evidenced by these preliminary changes observed by Kubler-Ross that occur while living, and many other cultures that have studied this process. So all this seems to be pointing in an interesting direction and how all of this might assist in the evolution of human consciousness.

Where to From Here?

In the long view, we are who we are, and we are each at the level of understanding that is right and correct for us at this point in our evolution. Whatever endpoint we arrive at as a group, total annihilation or transcendence to a level of consciousness that integrates both intellect and compassion, cause and intention drives progress down either road. Either result is fine, energy can be neither created nor destroyed, if the former road is taken, then we will just continue the story somewhere else.

There is another theme here that I have tried to elaborate upon, that our intention drives our reality. This is not a new idea, many have talked about it, but may require a deeper understanding that our intentions can have effects that are as far-reaching as the creation of the universe itself. There is the yin and the yang, the balance and connectedness of the nature of this reality that has been so far missed in this age and culture; that an individual can, at pivotal moments, be an agent of change through the energies of compassion, forgiveness and acceptance. Better still, we may be hard-wired to do so, and we must all achieve it to evolve as a species. Could our surrender to the transcendent, a refinding of the Sacred, be necessary for that change?

References

Altea, R. (1995). *The Eagle and the Rose.* New York: Warner Books.

Aurobindo, S. (2009). *The Hidden Forces of Life.* Pondicherry: Sri Aurobindo Ashram.

Beck, D & Cowan, C. (1996). *Spiral Dynamics: Mastering Values, Leadership and Change.* Blackwell: Cornwall UK.

Brennan, B. (1988). *Hands of Light.* New York: Bantam Books.

Brennan, B. (1993). *Light Emerging.* New York: Bantam Books.

Dalia Lama (2003). *Mind of Clear Light: Advice on Dying and Living a Better Life.* New York: Atria Books.

Eliade, M. (2004). *Shamanism: Archaic Techniques of Ecstasy.* Princeton: Princeton University Press.

Goldhaber, D. (2000). *Theories of Human Development: An Integrative Perspective.* New York: Wiley.

Greene, B. (1999). *The Elegant Universe.* New York: First Vintage Books.

Grof, S. (1993). *The Holotropic Mind: The Three Levels of Human Consciousness and How They Shape Our Lives.* New York: Harper Collins.New York: Harper Collins.

Hall, C. & Nordby, V J. (1973). *A Primer of Jungian Psychology.* New York: Mentor.

Harner, M. (1990). *The Way of the Shaman.* San Francisco: HarperCollins.

Hunt, V. (1989). *Infinite Mind.* Malibu, CA: Malibu Publishing.

Jones, W.T. (1969). *Hobbes to Hume: A History of Western Philosophy.* San

Francisoco: Harcourt, Brace and World.

Jung, C., Yates, J., ed. (1999). *Jung on Death and Immortality.* Princeton: Princeton University Press.

Kubler-Ross, E. (1969). *On Death and Dying.* New York: Macmillan Publishing Co.

Lauf, D. (1977). *Secret Doctrines of the Tibetan Books of the Dead.* New York: Shambala.

Laughlin, C.D., McManus, J. and d'Aquili, E.G. (1990). *Brain, Symbol and Experience: Towards a Neurophenomenology of Human Consciousness.* Boston: Shambala.

Maslow, A. (1970). *Toward Being a Person.* New York: Wiley.

Myss, C. (1996). *Anatomy of the Spirit.* New York: Three Rivers Press.

Neihardt, J. (1988). *Black Elk Speaks: Being the Life Story of a Holy Man of the Oglala Sioux.* Lincoln NE: University of Nebraska Press.

Noel, D. C. (1997). *The Soul of Shamanism.* New York: Continuum.

Rinpoche, S. (1993). *The Tibetan Book of Living and Dying.* New York: Harper Collins.

Rock, A.J. & Krippner, S. (2011). *Demystifying Shamans and their World: A Multidisciplinary Study.* Exeter, UK: Imprint Academic.

Tiller, W.A. et al. (2001). *Conscious Acts of Creation.* Walnut Creak CA: Pavior Publishing.

Tiller, W.A. (1997). *Science and Human Transformation: Subtle Energies, Intentionality and Consciousness.* Walnut Creek, CA: Pavior Publishing.

Townsend, J.B. (2005). Individualist Religious Movements: Core and Neo-shamanism. *Anthropology of Consciousness 15* 1 1-9.

Trungpa, C & Fremantle, F., translators. (2000). *The Tibetan Book of the Dead.*

Boston: Shambala.

Trungpa, C. (1992). *Transcending Madness: The Experience of the Six Bardos.* Boston: Shambala.

Wade, J. (1996). *Changes of Mind: A Holonomic Theory of the Evolution of Consciousness.* Albany: State University of New York Press.

Winkelman, M. (2002). Shamanic Universals and Evolutionary Psychology (1). *Journal of Ritualistic Studies* 16:2 63-76.

Winkelman, M. (2002). Shamanism and Cognitive Evolution. *Cambridge Archeological Journal.* 12:1 71-101.

Winkelman, M. (2010). *Shamanism: A Biopsychosocial Paradigm of Consciousness and Healing.* Santa Barbara, CA: Praeger.

Wilber, K. (1996) *A Brief History of Everything.* Boston: Shambala.

Wilber, K. (2000) *Integral Psychology: Consciousness, Spirit, Psychology, Therapy.* Boston: Shambala.

About Elena Gillespie

Elena Gillespie is a research investigator in traumatic brain injury in the Midwest. She has earned her B.S. in molecular biology and her PhD. in Human Development. This book is based upon the work of her dissertation. She came into transpersonal work and investigating numinous experience by accidentally healing her dog of cancer.

She has conducted and published research in the application of Reiki, a hands-on healing modality, in the management of pain in diabetic painful neuropathy at the University of Michigan, and was co-founder of the NIH-funded Alternative Medicine Research Center (UM CAMRC). She currently works at Saybrook University in California. Her current research interest is in the use of meditation for emotional regulation in patients who have suffered a traumatic brain injury. She lives in Indiana with her partner Steve and their five finches, Henry, Nora, Audrey, Sam and Janey.

Synopsis of Future Work

Elena Gillespie's next project will be a further exploration of her psychic and mediumship vision and healing work. Modern physics currently can show no proof of the multidimensionality of the universe, but perhaps we have been looking in the wrong direction, the various levels of reality are perceived from within the human mind. Currently she is recounting many of these on her blog, *A Farther Axis*:

http://fartheraxis.com/

If you liked this work, please leave a review for her on her Book page in Amazon.

www.ingramcontent.com/pod-product-compliance
Lightning Source LLC
Chambersburg PA
CBHW060510030426
42337CB00015B/1836